TRAVELS
OF A
LONDON SCHOOLBOY

The Pocock and Kennedy families playing charades at the home of John Kennedy in Burton Crescent, near today's Euston Road. Painted by Henry Andrews and exhibited at the Royal Academy in 1833, the scene is the execution of Mary Queen of Scots. Lewis Pocock (John's cousin) plays the chaplain and the artist stands by the window as the executioner. In the audience John Kennedy and his wife are seated in the centre; Samuel Pocock stands on the far right and Thomas Pocock, the lawyer, stands on the left of the back row of spectators.

TRAVELS
OF A
LONDON SCHOOLBOY
1826 - 1830
John Pocock's diary of life in London
and voyages to Cape Town and the
Swan River Settlement

edited by
Tom Pocock

with research by
Marjorie Holder

HISTORICAL PUBLICATIONS

First published 1996
by Historical Publications Ltd
32 Ellington Street, London N7 8PL
(Tel: 0171-607 1628)

ISBN 0 948667 35 4
A catalogue record for this book is available from the British Library

Typeset in Palatino by Historical Publications Ltd
Reproduction by G & J Graphics Ltd, London EC1
Printed by Edelvives, Zaragoza, Spain

Contents

1. John Thomas Pocock painted in Cape Town, c.1840. Artist unknown.

Introduction

by Marjorie Holder

One Sunday afternoon in the autumn of 1826, George and Hannah Pocock were relaxing in their large, comfortable house which George, a speculative builder, had designed and placed with others on the outskirts of Kilburn – just three miles north of London along the road to Edgware – in those days a pretty village. Their small children played happily. An older boy, at a loss for something to do, began to write:

'Made up my mind to keep a daily journal of any occurrences of note and so I got Papa's old banking account book and began upon the leaves which had not been written upon...'

Just over three years later he was writing in a sailing ship which pitched and rolled as it rounded the Needles rocks into the stormy January sea towards the Atlantic. Holding on hard in the heavy swell and clutching his quill, he carefully inscribed:

Left Portsmouth about 2 o'clk when the owner left us and also the pilot soon after we passed the Warner Buoy after clearing the Isle of Wight. I soon lost sight (perhaps for ever) of my native land.

Our diarist, John Thomas Pocock, had quaintly told us he was 'aged eleven and three-quarters' when he began to tell the story of his life day by day for nearly half a century.

At first, John failed to give his background clearly (and what youngster could be expected to explain it for unknown readers countless years afterwards?) and he recorded his father's financial crisis in code. The gregarious Pococks had friends and relations as numerous as the characters in a Russian novel and it has been difficult to disentangle them. Fortunately we are helped by an elegiac essay on the life of his father written about ten years later. Taken together, the diary and the afterthoughts he added in 1835 give a positive picture of London and people in late Regency days, so often omitted by historians who hurry us on to Victorian times. Little did he know how much he was adding to history as he began the detailed contemporary account of his life unbiased by repeated memory or modern distortion.

The family we meet through his pages was one of those who found prosperity in the expansion of Georgian London. George Pocock's great-grandfather, Charles, born about 1673, had come to the capital from Berkshire in 1740, and is described as a maltster of Greenham. He settled in Shoreditch, to the east of the City, bought land, designed and built houses for sale, then repeating the process in Islington, Southwark and Marylebone. Later George himself concentrated on the pleasant hillside country to the north-west of Kilburn village towards Hampstead. John gives a happy picture of early days there, describing how he played in the 'Hilly Field' and paddled in the 'Kil-bourne' brook. In his memoir he remembers: *'Let me see, there was fat Punch and Bull and Lobster and the black horse who lost his sight and whom Punch used to lead about the fields....one of the finest teams of horses for miles around'*. He blames his father's easy-going nature for the decline in the business, but, unknown to the little boy, George must have been affected by the serious commercial panic in the City which began in 1825, just before John started writing. Numerous banks had closed and there were many bankruptcies because of the activities of 'bubble' companies. George's case was no exception – indeed the great Charles Dickens's father, John, was incarcerated for a similar debt.

Within his own family, John's father does not seem to have been a strong character but his mother certainly was. She was its firm foundation and I feel sure we can hear her voice in some of her son's opinions. His elder brother was George Felix, aged seventeen, who had emigrated a year before to enlist in the East India Company's St Helena Artillery. He seldom wrote to his doting parents who worried about him constantly and he lost touch with John in later days. The gap in ages was marked because two sisters had died of whooping cough in 1813, while still toddlers. John Thomas's arrival on 12 December 1814 must have been a great joy to his bereaved parents.

Other members of that close and loving family were Emily Eden and Eliza Kilburn aged nine and six, his constant playmates at that time.

Seldom mentioned is Thomas who seems to have been a quiet child aged five. A letter to Cape Town from Mama tells of his death in 1834 '*....a long expected event and a most painful subject, my mother does not enter into particulars.*' writes John. Also present were Lewis Grevillle ('Little Lew') and Maria Hannah aged three and two respectively. Maria was known as 'baby' until replaced by a sister, Betsy, whom we never meet as John left home soon after her birth.

But it is Lewis Greville, born on 19 February, 1823, who figures so largely in John's life. They were obviously devoted and we read how John carried

Lew when he was about four years old, nearly eight miles back home to Kilburn from Southwark....'*He being too fat to walk so long a distance!*' The night before John parted from his heart-broken family to go to Australia he writes, '*Slept with dear little Lewis who cuddled me, he said, for the last time.*'

The most historical and fascinating periods of John's earlier life are given in his graphic description of the adventurous journey to his new homeland. He was apprenticed, after his father, George's, tragic death, to a surgeon, by George's kind brother John Thomas snr, whom he calls 'My good Uncle and Namesake'. The surgeon was about to emigrate to the Swan River Colony, newly formed in 1829. It was so well advertised that several thousand would-be inhabitants were pouring there, to find no facilities ready for them. Friends have shown great interest when I have told them how John arrived at Fremantle and Perth, to a bleak storm-bound shore – scattered with wrecks, and little to eat but their own ship's hard tack while they built tents for shelter.

The surgeon, Mr Carter, taught John the 'art and mystery' of his trade while acting as the medical officer on the passenger ship to Australia. Some of the cures of that day must have had the opposite effect to that intended!

According to to an official history of the Swan River Settlement, many people were warned of the bad conditions and we note that the Carters changed their mind – pregnant Mrs Carter remained behind when they called at Cape Town, but her husband had to fulfil his contract with the ship's owner to complete the voyage, finding his own way back. He took Johnson, his manservant, and John with him. There was delay in finding a passage, so the youngster had much excitement exploring unkown territory. He sailed back eventually via Mauritius in a couple of battered little brigs. John and the surgeon both had scurvy, in the awful conditions so brilliantly described.

Twelve years later he was joined in Cape Town by his brother Lewis, 'Little Lew', my maternal great-grandfather, but they did not recognise each other after so long a time. John remarks how tall Lew had grown. But it was again John who had to 'carry' his brother through many troubles. Lew amuses us with his own diary of voyaging to the Cape, quoted later.

I came across the diary through a South African cousin, the late Myrtle Greville Pocock (Mrs Ashworth), who placed the carefully preserved journals and letter-books in the South African Library, Cape Town, and published an account of John's later life.

She faithfully transcribed his early years and sent them to me. Then, by strange fortune, I discovered another member of the London branch of the family, Hugh Shellshear Pocock, the editor, publisher and genealogist – whose ancestor was no less than John's 'Good Uncle and Namesake', the wealthy business man, owner of St Bride's Wharf in the City through which he imported timber and coal. As the diary tells us, he also was a close neighbour at Kilburn, having a country house built by John's father in Greville Place – the name taken by so many of the first Lewis Greville's offspring under the impression it was a family surname. Hugh knew all the early history of the Pococks, but had long been seeking the destiny of George's family. We waited excitedly for each instalment from Cape Town as Greville Ashworth unfolded the story, so that I could decipher the coded passages and research the background.

Now I have been lucky in persuading yet another cousin descended from 'Good Uncle John', to use his professional skills in editing this fascinating voice from the past. Not only has he an intimate knowledge of the London of John Pocock, but has studied the sea-life of those days as his books about Nelson and his times tell us. I thank the well-known author and journalist, Tom Pocock.

Oh, I forgot Emily! She gave me my middle name, Emily.

Editor's Note

When John Pocock transcribed his diary in a fair hand in 1835, after he had settled in Cape Town, he carefully marked additions made with hindsight and these, as will be seen, have been kept separate. His narrative has been edited, omitting the more mundane entries and references to some people whose occupation, or relationship to the author, is not given. Here and there his punctuation has been slightly amended.

Much of the London diary was published in paperback form by the Camden History Society in 1980 as *The Diary of a London Schoolboy, 1826-1830*. Then, the footnotes and editing were by Lady Holder, Mrs Christina Gee and Christopher Wade, whose work has been drawn upon in this edition, and to whom I am most grateful. Now this fuller edition includes John's account of his voyages to the Cape of Good Hope and Australia and his young brother Lewis's voyage to Cape Town twelve years later, together with their first impressions of life there. Our gratitude is also due to Mr. Ronald Evans of Harare, Zimbabwe; Professor John Pocock; Michael Pocock; Dr Karel Schoeman, Head of Special Collections at the South African Library, Cape Town, where John Pocock's original diary is kept, and Hugh Watson.

John's later diary of his life at the Cape was edited by another member of their family, Greville Ashworth, and published as *The Life and Fortunes of John Pocock of Cape Town, 1814-76* by the College Tutorial Press of Cape Town in 1974.

Tom Pocock

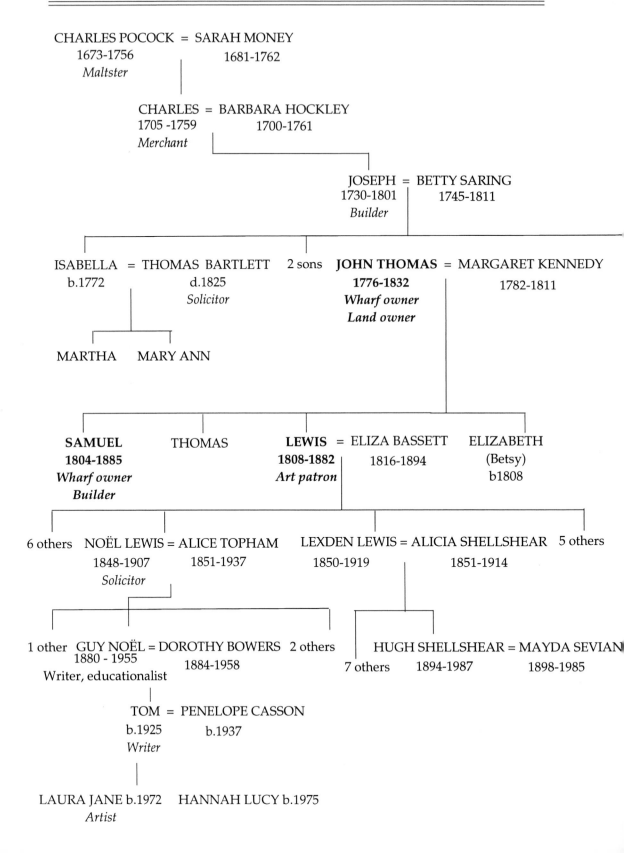

CHARLES POCOCK = SARAH MONEY
1673-1756   1681-1762
Maltster

CHARLES = BARBARA HOCKLEY
1705 -1759   1700-1761
Merchant

JOSEPH = BETTY SARING
1730-1801   1745-1811
Builder

ISABELLA = THOMAS BARTLETT   2 sons   **JOHN THOMAS** = MARGARET KENNEDY
b.1772   d.1825   **1776-1832**   1782-1811
                Solicitor   ***Wharf owner***
                                          Land owner

MARTHA   MARY ANN

SAMUEL   THOMAS   **LEWIS** = ELIZA BASSETT   ELIZABETH
1804-1885   **1808-1882** | 1816-1894   (Betsy)
Wharf owner   ***Art patron***   b1808
Builder

6 others   NOËL LEWIS = ALICE TOPHAM   LEXDEN LEWIS = ALICIA SHELLSHEAR   5 others
           1848-1907   1851-1937   1850-1919   1851-1914
           Solicitor

1 other   GUY NOËL = DOROTHY BOWERS   2 others   HUGH SHELLSHEAR = MAYDA SEVIAN
          1880 - 1955   1884-1958   7 others   1894-1987   1898-1985
          Writer, educationalist

TOM = PENELOPE CASSON
b.1925   b.1937
Writer

LAURA JANE b.1972   HANNAH LUCY b.1975
Artist

POCOCK FAMILY TREE

(Branches connected with this diary)

Based on research by Hugh Pocock

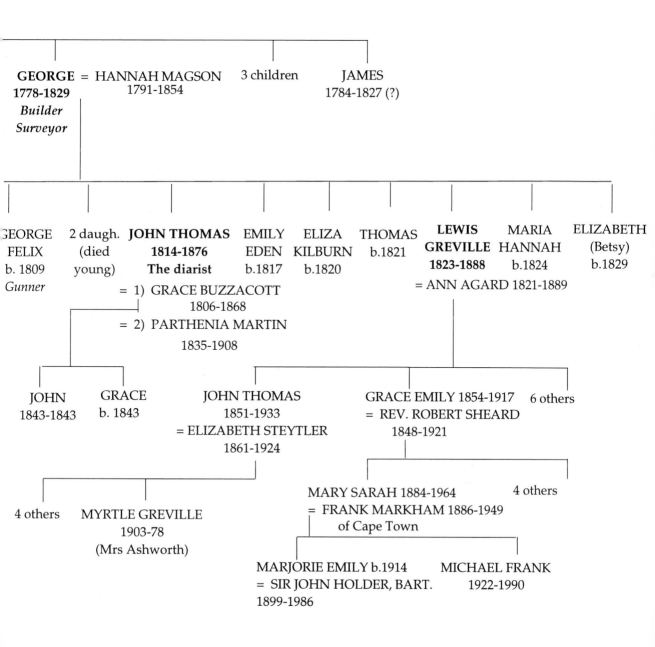

GEORGE = HANNAH MAGSON   3 children   JAMES
1778-1829   1791-1854   1784-1827 (?)
Builder
Surveyor

GEORGE   2 daugh.   **JOHN THOMAS**   EMILY   ELIZA   THOMAS   **LEWIS**   MARIA   ELIZABETH
FELIX   (died   **1814-1876**   EDEN   KILBURN   b.1821   **GREVILLE**   HANNAH   (Betsy)
b. 1809   young)   **The diarist**   b.1817   b.1820   **1823-1888**   b.1824   b.1829
Gunner   = ANN AGARD 1821-1889

= 1) GRACE BUZZACOTT
1806-1868
= 2) PARTHENIA MARTIN
1835-1908

JOHN   GRACE   JOHN THOMAS   GRACE EMILY 1854-1917   6 others
1843-1843   b. 1843   1851-1933   = REV. ROBERT SHEARD
= ELIZABETH STEYTLER   1848-1921
1861-1924

4 others   MYRTLE GREVILLE   MARY SARAH 1884-1964   4 others
1903-78   = FRANK MARKHAM 1886-1949
(Mrs Ashworth)   of Cape Town

MARJORIE EMILY b.1914   MICHAEL FRANK
= SIR JOHN HOLDER, BART.   1922-1990
1899-1986

Chapter One

At Home in London

(Born 12th December, 1814 - aged 11¾)

29 OCT 1826, Sunday
Made up my mind to keep a daily journal of any occurrences of note and so I got Papa's old banking account book and began upon the leaves which had not been written upon.

James Magson [*his mother's young half-brother*] to dinner, after which we youngsters mustered sixpence to buy fruit. Mr. Jeffries came in the evening. Papa fell asleep and Mama determined upon teasing him by tickling his nose with a pen which made us laugh very much. James stayed with us all night.

30 OCT
Went with Papa and James Magson to town in the morning. Papa sent me to Newgate Market after which I went to Uncle's [*John Thomas Pocock, his uncle, the owner of St Bride's Wharf, where he had lived since 1806, on the Thames below Fleet Street, and imported timber and coal. After a disastrous fire in 1810 it was rebuilt and named Phoenix Wharf*] who seemed very kind. Called on Gurney's [*Captain William Gurney, the owner of Peele's Coffee House and hotel, 177-8 Fleet Street on the corner of Fetter Lane. Frequented by lawyers, it kept files of newspapers; Peele's survived as pub until road widening, c.1970*] and then walked home.

31 OCT
Stayed at home all day. Emily [*sister*] brought home another dog....

1 NOV
Mr Green [*Paddington grocer*] came in the morning and offered me another dog. Sarah Yates, Capt. Gurney's servant, called and told me Tom Gurney is coming on Saturday next to spend a few days with us. The two Miss Rogers [*daughters of the family doctor*] called in the evening and played at whist with us after tea – their brother fetched them home. N.B. Plenty of dogs.

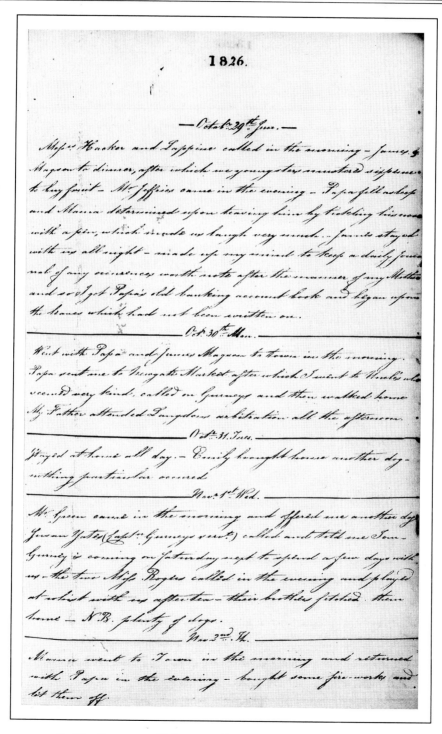

2. *The first page of John Pocock's diary as transcribed in 1835.*

3. St Bride's Wharf seen from the southern end of Blackfriars Bridge; from Barker's Panorama of London, 1792.

2 NOV

Mama went to Town in the morning and returned with Papa in the evening – bought some fireworks and let them off.

3 NOV

I was swinging in the garden between two large elms in the morning when Fred Gurney came in quite unexpectedly to spend the day with me. He stayed all night intending to return early in the morning.

4 NOV

A very wet morning, Fred and I went to Paddington and back; I broke a wine glass, had a tap on the head and a long lecture from Mama for taking some gunpowder out of the storeroom cupboard. Emily too was beaten. All very dull in the midst of which Fred went.

5 NOV, Sunday

A miserably wet Sunday, Papa and I walked to Tottenham Court Road, thence to Camden Town and from Camden Town to Hampstead, we were thoroughly soaked through and I was nearly drowned in *Pond* Street. Uncle J. Magson came to dinner and remained all night.

4. Pond Street, Hampstead, c.1830, where the diarist 'nearly drowned'.

6 NOV
Mrs. Jay came to tea. The children, Sarah Yates and self went up the village to see the fire-works, Guy Fawkes Day having been kept to-day as yesterday was Sunday. A sham battle was very well kept up by the boys who divided in two companies on either side the Kil-bourne and assailed each other with squibs, crackers, etc.

7 NOV
Went to St. Bride's in the morning stayed to dinner and tea with my good Uncle and namesake John Thomas Pocock. Very frosty evening, returned home with Papa.

8 NOV
At home the whole day, our garden looks bare – nothing particular occurred.

9 NOV
Lord Mayor's Day, walked to my Uncle's at the Wharf to see the show by water with my Father and sisters, where we spent a very pleasant day. I was one of the party who went in my Uncle's boat after the Stationers' Company's barge, my Uncle being one of their company. We were treated with the greatest kindness; called at Peele's on our return and left Eliza [*sister*] with her playfellow Mary Gurney.

11 NOV

My Father arrested this morning. To Mr. Mortimer, Albany and Carter, Bear St. in the morning with my Father, thence to Carey Street. [*Thomas Hill Mortimer, attorney of 4 Albany Court Yard, Piccadilly, made loans to George Pocock at high interest, which "completely fettered his estate", resulting in his arrest for debt. He also owned property on the Greville Hill estate and the names Mortimer Crescent and Mortimer Place survive near Greville Road and Kilburn Priory.*] Afterwards to Bewley [*another business associate*], Newgate Market – called at Gurney's on my return home.

12 NOV, Sunday

Papa at Banco Regis [*the King's Bench Prison off Borough High Street in Southwark. The most comfortable of the debtors' prisons in London, with a complete community of a chapel, two pubs, a coffee house and food stalls within the walls. It was known as "the most delightful place of incarceration in London". There were 224 apartments and the social classes could be kept largely separate, the more affluent, like George Pocock, being able to purchase occasional day leave. In the slump of December 1825, the prison was crowded when more than 100,000 writs for debt were issued in England*]. Maria [*baby sister*] fell down stairs in the morning, but was not hurt much, her head being much fortified. A Mrs. Heard called in the afternoon [*Mrs Heard was the landlady of Heard's lodging house in Serle's Court, or Place, off Carey Street, Lincoln's Inn, where George Pocock was to stay after his arrest on 8 November 1826*].

5. The King's Bench Prison in 1823.

13 Nov

Went to my Father and remained with him all the morning, he seemed very dull. Took tea with my Uncle and slept at Gurney's.

14 Nov

Spent the morning pleasantly at Peele's and returned home to the Priory in the afternoon.

15 Nov

Took Edward Kingcombe home to Battersea in the afternoon and at the invitation of his mother I remained there all night.

16 Nov

Walked with Mr. Kingcombe to Southwark to see my Father who had gone home. Took tea at Peele's and returned home.

17 Nov

My Mother went to the City in the morning and brought home my first volume of Dolly's *British Theatre* from Stevens the binder in Marylebone Lane.

18 Nov

At home all day – hired a new servant with a *new face* which I detest.

19 Nov

A very dull day. James Magson to dinner, he remained all night.

20 Nov

James went to town with my Father and returned in the aftn. Mr. Dickens having settled for the land. Papa picked out some gown pieces for my Mother and Sisters rather ugly.

22 Nov

Our new servant came. To Paddington in the evening.

23 Nov

My Mother went to the City in the afternoon and unfortunately lost a £10 note in the road. Mr. Lucas the Solicitor and his son called in the afternoon.

25 Nov

To Ellis, Ludgate Hill, then to Gurney's. Emily and Eliza accompanied my Mother to town.

6. St Bride's Church, Fleet Street; by Thomas H. Shepherd, 1829

26 NOV, Sunday
Mr Crutchley [*possibly G.F. Cruchley, the cartographer, of 81 Fleet Street*] came in the morning, also James Magson. My friends Tom and Fred Gurney arrived just in dinner time. Papa and Mr. Kingcombe coming also, made a pretty good party. James and I went part of the way home with the Gurneys.

27 NOV
Went with James to Grays Inn Lane in the morning where we met Mr. and Mrs. Kingcombe and Mr. Jay. I then went to Paddington from there with Mrs. K. to her home in Battersea Square where my Mother came as appointed and played a rubber at whist.

28 NOV
Walked to Battersea and back home; my Mother having left her reticule [*handbag*] behind her.

30 NOV
Mrs. and Mrs. Mitchell called in the evening and remained all night. These are folks I am not very fond of.

1 DEC
Sister Emily's birthday. Miss Annie Rogers spent the afternoon with us and we had a fine game in the 'long parlour'. My Father returned in the evening from Worcester, he has visited Stratford-on-Avon during the journey, and visited the house where the immortal Shakespeare was born.

2 DEC
Had a long and muddy walk in the morning to Mr. Walmesley, Acton Green, rode to Smithfield with Mr. W. where we met my Father, had tea there, called on Mr. Gurney and then went home.

3 DEC, Sunday
Mr. and Mrs. Kingcombe to dinner, also James Magson. Mr. Jeffries (the *nine cup* tea drinker) came to tea. My father walked home with Mr. K.

5 DEC
Father and James to town on business. Poor little Tom and Lew are laid up with the scarlet fever. Anne Rogers came to spend the aftn. with Emily.

6 DEC
James went to Limehouse for my Father. At home all day.

7 DEC
My Father and James went to Town together in the morning. At home taking care of Tom and Lew who are better.

8 DEC
My Father and James went to the City to meet Bewley to arrange some business. James returned in the afternoon.

That infamous rascal Bewley arrested my Father and lodged him at 'Heard's', Serles Court.

9 DEC
Walked with Emily to Brixton to see Mrs. Underwood – returning we took tea at Gurney's.

An incident occurred on the road which I shall remember as long as I live, trivial as it was, for it impressed me with a lively sense of my dear sister's generosity and good nature – about this time I obtained and merited the reproach of being very

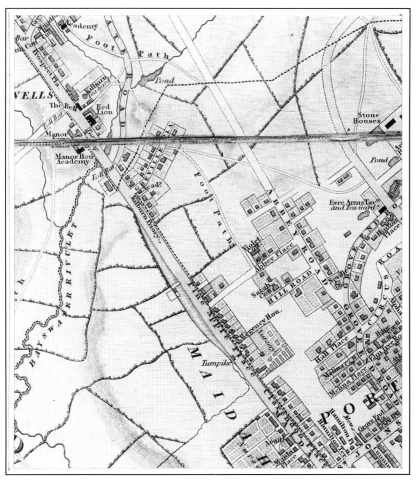

7. *The Kilburn area of the Edgware Road in Cruchley's map of 1833.*
Greville Place is to the top left.

stingy. When near Kennington we were both rather hungry and I purchased *six* small biscuits in the Lambeth Road and offered her *two* which she gladly accepted, remarking with great good humour "that she only expected one"; stung to the soul with this just rebuke, although it was not intended as such, I instantly offered another biscuit but could not persuade her to take it, alleging that she was sure I was more hungry than herself.

10 Dec, Sunday
To church in the morning. James went to see my Father.

8. The last of the family home. A surviving and much-altered fragment of 7 Kilburn Priory (now 136 Maida Vale), where the Pococks lived, in 1995. The plaque commemorates a later resident, William Friese-Greene, the pioneer of cinematography.

11 DEC

My Mother, James and myself went to Serle's Place in the morning returning at night. Saw Messrs. Murrell, Gurney and Underwood there.

12 DEC

I am twelve years old this day. Mr. and Mrs. Kingcombe came to dinner. Mr. Mitchell and wife 'dropped in' as the saying is, in the morning and put my mother to great inconvenience in providing a bed for them.

14 DEC

With Magson early to Serle's Place, from thence to Limehouse to see the Holmes, returned home very tired.

15 DEC

At home greater part of the day. Our servant Mary's sister died at Middlesex Hospital this day.

17 DEC, Sunday

Mr. and Mrs. Paine recently from St. Helena called in the afternoon and amused us with many anecdotes about George [*George Felix Pocock, John's elder brother, had enlisted in the East India Company's St. Helena Artillery*]. Mr. P. had a fine romp with Eliza.

The various labels on the map read:

N, W, E, S

The Hilly Field

No 6

No 6

Greville Place

Kilburn Priory

Kilburn Priory

A View of the Neighbourhood of No 6 Greville Place —1828—

eric fraser

The Bell Inn

9. *The Pocock estate at Kilburn Priory in 1828, drawn by Eric Fraser, c.1980. The diarist's uncle, John Pocock, owned No. 6 Greville Place, which survives as No. 18.*

18 DEC

My Mother went to the City in Humphries' stage in the morning. To old *Vere* the *dear* grocer in aftn.

19 DEC

Very cold frost weather, at home all day.

20 DEC

My Mother to Serle's Place and remained in Town all night. House very lonely without her.

22 DEC

To Peele's in the morning for Emily with whom I returned home after dinner.

23 DEC

Came home from Town with my Mother, and bought the fruit for Christmas Day on the road.

25 DEC

Had a new suit of clothes this day, spent the day and a very pleasant evening at Gurney's with my Mother and sister: we children did justice to the plumb pudding.

26 DEC

With my Father all the morning from whom I returned home in the afternoon.

27 DEC

Went to the Gurneys for the purpose of fetching Tom, Fred and their sisters, who returned with me to spend a day or two at the Priory [*the Pocock house*].

28 DEC

Spent a very pleasant day with my young playmates. Mrs. Gurney in the afternoon. We all played at Pope Joan [*a card game*], after which singing was introduced. Mrs. Jay tormented us with some ugly old songs. Mary Gurney sang, *In my Cottage near a Road* very well.

30 DEC

Tom and George with me all day, rambling about the fields, village, etc.

31 DEC, Sunday

To church with my two sisters, Lewis and Thomas. Lew diverted my Mother by saying he set up a large, pretty pin-cushion in church.

Chapter Two

A Schoolboy in London

1 JAN 1827

Tom went home with James in the morning – amused myself by sticking in theatrical characters into an old copy book.

5 JAN

Frederick, Duke of York, died this day. Went to Jools [*possibly Joe's coffee house in Mitre Court, Fleet Street*] with Mama, saw John Gosling, brought John Kingcombe home with us.

6 JAN

Twelve cake day ['*Twelfth Night' after Christmas*]. My Mother and James came home in the evening and brought me a piece of cake and ornament sent by Mrs. Gurney.

8 JAN

To Town early, walked with Fred Gurney to Mr. Bethel, Camden Town, and slept with him at Peele's.

9 JAN

To the Session House, Clerkenwell to find Gray, but could not. Walked to Limehouse with Magson and home at night.

10 JAN

To my Father – got wet through on the road.

11 JAN

Took George Kingcombe home to Battersea, from there I walked to my Father.

12 JAN

With James Magson to Town, wished him a hearty farewell as he goes to Chatham to-day, previous to setting out for St. Helena to join my brother in the E.I.C. Artillery.

13 JAN

My Mother went to Town and I to Paddington, where I assisted a poor old man along, affected with palsy. Capt. Gurney, having sold Peele's Coffee House, removed to-day in lodgings in a comfortable house in Upper Rosamond Street, Clerkenwell.

14 JAN, Sunday
Very dull, gloomy day, no visiting on that account.

15 JAN
Walked to the City with my Mother and Sisters. We called at the Wharf and saw my cousin Lewis [*the third son of John's uncle, John Thomas Pocock, then two days short of his nineteenth birthday; he was to become a notable patron of the arts and founder of the Art Union for the promotion of the arts*], returned p.m.

16 JAN
To Hemps in the morning and remained there all night owing to the loss of ½ a sovereign which I dropped in the parlour and which I was confident was picked up by some of the party.

18 JAN
Went to Mr. Garrett [*James Garrett was proprietor of the Kingston House Academy, 30 Portland Terrace, Regent's Park*] with Mama who paid him £10. My Mother has been sadly grieved at my remaining from school the last quarter. I am to return on Monday as a day scholar.

20 JAN
With my Mother, Sisters and Mary to see the procession attending the Duke of York's funeral on its route from London to Windsor, but we arrived on the road too late. There were thousands of disappointed spectators like ourselves on the road, every Inn seemed full. We, however, got admission into one where we took some refreshment and were much delighted in hearing a man sing *Pat Denny and his Pig*. My Mother with her usual good nature to make up for our disappointment took us in to Mrs. Kingcombe with whom, and the young folk, we spent a very happy evening.

21 JAN
We went to Serle's Place but my Father had left.

22 JAN
Went to school in the morning and got through my tasks pretty well.

23 JAN
To school as usual – we have some famous singers amongst the boys: there is

10. *Lewis Pocock, John's first cousin, painted by Henry Andrews, 1833.*

Braham [*John Braham (1774-1856), celebrated singer in opera; owned the Colosseum, Regent's Park and built the St James's Theatre*] and Sophia's son and Miss Stevens' [*Catherine Stevens (1794-1856), actress and singer acting at the Theatre Royal, Drury Lane, in 1827*] nephs.

25 JAN
To my Father after school (Banco Regis). The two Miss Gurneys came to spend a day or two with us.

28 JAN, Sunday
Cold wet day. Took the Miss Gurneys home: went to my Father with Fred. Called on my Uncle who was rather cross owing perhaps to the thaw.

29 JAN
At home all day writing a long letter to my brother George.

1 FEB
To school as usual. Old Monk [*a teacher*] is a queer one.

2 FEB
To Charing Cross with my Mother very early in the morning where we met Mrs. Kingcombe, saw them off in the Chatham Stage. Mrs. K. unfortunately dropped her pocket pistol which being made of brandy and glass could not stand the shock. My Mother has gone to see James Magson previous to his leaving England. Went on to see my Father and home in the evening.

5 FEB
To school in the morning, rather late which makes me behindhand in the class.

8 FEB
Went to school and afterwards to my Father. Met the Miss Gurneys and Emily opposite Portman Place going to Kilbourne, to-day being Eliza's birthday.

11 FEB, Sunday
Went on the brook sliding with Fred in the morning. My Mother went to Southwark. Went with him to Pineapple Gate [*there was a Pine Apple Toll Bar and a Pine Apple Place in Edgware Road near Kilburn Priory*] on his return home.

13 FEB
To school very late again. Got a sound scholding notwithstanding my 8¾ ticket [*probably leave of absence until 8.45am*].

15 FEB

To my Father in the morning. Met Mr. Gurney near Marylebone New Church, and found him, his lady and Mr. and Mrs. Kingcombe on my return home having a rubber of whist.

17 FEB

Went to my Father and called for Tom Gurney who came home with me, intending to remain to-morrow with us. Received a very pretty Valentine by post in the evening.

18 FEB

After dinner my Mother, Tom Gurney and self walked to the Serpentine River in Hyde Park and were much amused by the skaters, many of whom received innumerable thumps on the upper story from the ice.

19 FEB

Called upon Captn. Murray, Soho Square, with my Mother, on the way to Drury Lane Theatre in the afternoon. We got a comfortable seat. Saw the tragedy of *The Stranger*. Kean [*Edmund Kean (1787-1833)*] performed very badly. The afterpiece was excellent, namely, *The Man in the Moon*. My Mother I am grieved to see did not enjoy the performance at all, her cares and woes are too many for her to be happy.

21 FEB

To school. The poor dolt, Tom Atkinson, had a sound hiding.

22 FEB

Poor old Andrew Richardson of Praed Street, Paddington died in Banco Regis this day. Went to school.

23 FEB

To school in the morning where the usual routine of Spelling, Reading, Writing, Cyphering, Burching and Caneing took place.

24 FEB

Half-holiday. Went with Emily to my Father. Saw Mr. Gurney there who persuaded Papa to let us dine with him in Rosamond Street, which we did. Emily stayed all night.

26 FEB

Mary [*probably Mary Gurney*] came to take Emily and Eliza to the Olympic Theatre [*in Maypole Alley, Drury Lane, which had opened in 1806*]. The pieces were *The Wild Boy of Bohemia* and a farce with which they were highly amused, especially Eliza.

11. St John's Wood Chapel, St John's Wood High Street, completed in 1814. It was designed by Thomas Hardwick.

28 FEB

To school, the minute hand of St. John's Wood Chapel pointing to twenty minutes past nine as usual.

2 MAR

Mr. Smith, a native of the Emerald Isle, and who has recently arrived from St. Helena, called in the morning. Went with him to my Father after dinner and remained all night. I witnessed in the evening an assemblage entitled a 'free and easy' but was so disgusted with it that I think this will be the *first* and *last* time I ever visit one.

3 MAR

Accompanied my Father to Guildhall where my Father was subpoenaed as witness in the case of Randall v Hoare and Co. [*The Courts of King's Bench and Common Pleas, where the case would have been heard, were in Guildhall Yard. The figures of the mythical giants Gog and Magog, carved in 1708, stood in the Guildhall.*] Plaintiff gained the cause. I was much amused with the J.A.W. of the Counsel pro and con. Visited Gog and Magog. This is my Mother's birthday.

6 MAR

To school, find it impossible to arrive there at the proper time owing to long distance from home. This is a great drawback to my advancement in study.

7 MAR

To Kingston House, *long last* as usual, feel perfectly convinced I am quite a dunce and shall probably remain so.

8 MAR

To school, as usual. Have a perfect hatred towards Regent's Park and environs. My old friend James Artis far excels me in learning, and·yet we began Latin together, are the same age within one day, etc.

9 MAR

Emily met me in the Park Road and took my books home, while I went to my Father, when I saw Mr. Gurney and Tom, came part of the way home with them.

10 MAR

Dragged along to school. George Bridgman, Jennings, Kynaston, Hendry, Page etc. *hoc genus omne* are all beating me hollow at Latin. Really I am quite discouraged.

11 MAR, Sunday

To Church like a good boy. At home remainder of the day.

12 MAR

To school. I have a great aversion to Mondays and Fridays, always blunder on those days more than on others.

13 MAR

On my return from school, Mama showed me a letter received from George. He was quite well but does not write very affectionately.

14 MAR

Went to school. Mrs. Garrett calls me "old steady".

18 MAR, Sunday

This morning I dropped the heavy shutter belonging to the stone kitchen on my foot which swelled seriously.

19 MAR

At home nursing my bad foot. Emily went to Garrett's and to Paddington.

20 MAR

Mama went to Gurneys then to Hocker's, and from there to my Father and came home very tired.

25 MAR, Sunday

Tom and Fred Gurney came in the morning and we spent a pleasant day together, my foot being much better, they returned in the evening.

27 MAR

Dreamed last night I shall not live a week, arose in good spirits at so good an omen. Mrs. Morgan from the Borough called and took dinner with us.

29 MAR

Walked in the morning to my Father. Remained with him during the day and called on my Uncle's returning, who behaved very kind to me.

2 APR

To school for the first time this fortnight on account of my foot. Mr. Murrell came in the evening and played off one of his eccentric tricks by bringing his *chops* in his pocket.

4 APR

Emily went to Paddington before breakfast to buy herself a slate. Mr. Grant, late of the East Indies, called in the evening. How very vain this man is, how very absurd.

6 APR

My Mother went to Town in the morning, she has a mortal aversion to high winds.

7 APR

Went to school. Mr. Mortimer called and Mama had some high words with him concerning the Greville Hill Estate.

10 APR

Some gentlemen called who wished to purchase our home, Papa's price is £1,900 stg. Mrs. Gurney and Ellen came in the evening, I was almost distracted with toothache and obliged to go to bed at 7 oclk.

11 APR

Mrs. Gurney went in the morning, Ellen stayed all day. George Kingcombe came to invite all the 'live stock' as his mother terms us to Battersea Fair on Monday next. Mr. Garrett gives a week's holiday this Easter. N.B. The cat had kittens to-day.

13 APR

Good Friday. Mama took Ellen Gurney home and Eliza with her who remained. Ellen is rather cross and pettish.

16 APR

Started early with Mary Gurney, Emily and Fred. Met my Mother and Eliza at Kingcombes', we enjoyed ourselves much in the Fair, seeing the shows and swinging etc., the fair is held in Battersea Square, right facing Mr. K's house.

17 APR

George Kingcombe ill in the morning in consequence of swinging. Mama bought many fairings [*china figurines*] for the young K's and sent me back with them. I was sulky all the morning, for I do not like Mrs. K's oddities, she is the very reverse of my Mother, bless her.

23 APR

Our house advertised to be sold by Public Auction sale to take place a fortnight. Papa intends selling off all his property on the Priory with the exception of the little cottage on Greville Hill into which we are to remove, our house being much too large for us.

24 APR

My mother attended the Vestry Meeting at the Marylebone Police Office concerning the Poor rates.

25 APR

Busy day at home, the charwoman ironing the whole of it.

26 APR

Went to Bethnall Green upon some peculiar business left unsettled by James Magson with his *Uncle,* then over old London Bridge [*Old London Bridge was about to be demolished; Sir John Rennie's new bridge was being built two hundred feet upstream and was to be opened in 1831*] to my Father. Mr. Williams the Mart auctioneer was there.

27 APR

James Keys our late carter went to Papa with a letter from my Mother and made a blunder by putting it in the Post Office.

28 APR

In terrible agony with the toothache, ran up the village almost mad to Dr. Rogers, who could not extract it.

29 APR, Sunday

Went in the morning to Papa who had gone to Chapel, my Father seemed unusually kind; Edward and George Kingcombe were at home when I came back. Uncle had been at our house and gave Emily a crown piece.

4 MAY

To school, fancy myself as a bit of a dunce.

5 MAY

Old Mr. Monk who has been so long away from our school came back to-day. Mr. Garrett turned him away for being drunk. This man once had the largest school in the metropolis before he took to drinking, he is a perfect master of seven languages and affords a lamentable instance of the misery produced by this degrading vice, for he has now scarcely a coat to his back.

7 MAY

I was with my Father at ½ past eight in the morning, came back again with Mr. Grant, called at his lodgings somewhere near the Holborn. Attended our sale at the Red Lion by Mr. Williams in the evening, the well and plot adjacent were sold to Mr. Mortimer. Mr. Shaw our neighbour of Abbey Cottage offered £1,200 for the house; Mr. and Mrs. Kingcombe, Mrs. Wright and Mr. Garrett came in the evening. Mrs. W. stayed all night.

9 MAY

With Mama to Town in the morning, while with Papa Mr. Murrell brought the deposit money from Williams.

13 MAY, Sunday

Went to Mr. Kingcombe in the morning, arrived there just in pudding time, after dinner we took a pleasant walk to Chelsea Reach and took some ale in the gardens of the 'Red House', a notable Inn and famous for that cowardly diversion 'pigeon shooting'. [*Originally Elizabethan, the Red House, a red-brick tavern was demolished before its Thames-side grounds were absorbed into Battersea Park.*]

15 MAY

Papa came to the Priory in the morning, went part of the way with him on his return to town. Papa treated me with some cyder.

16 MAY

Went in the morning to Serjeant's Inn [*one of the Inns of Court; in Chancery Lane*] where I met Papa and Mr. Murrell. Had some beef Alamode [*Beauf à la Mode, a beef stew*] for dinner. Papa dared me to have my tooth out, accordingly put my courage to the test and went with him to Hayes the celebrated dentist in Bedford Court, St. Martin's Lane, who took out my old tormentor. My first impression when he pulled it out was that he had *pulled my head off* instead of the tooth.

12. The Red House inn, Battersea, artist unknown. Watercolour c.1840

17 MAY

Found Fred Gurney at our house on my return from school. Papa came home in the evening, a very wet night, with thunder and lightning which prevented Fred going home.

19 MAY

Papa came in the afternoon, and I measured some land with him on Greville Hill adjoining Carpenter's House. Mr. Mortimer joined us. Emily and Eliza went to Paddington in the afternoon.

20 MAY, Sunday

Went to Mrs. Wright, Turner Street, Whitechapel in the morning, walked through the City. Nothing can exceed the miserable monotony and dead appearance of London on a Sunday, especially a wet Sunday. Saw Josiah [*Wright*] who went with his sister Caroline to take tea with her *affianced* Mr. Brown the worthy citizen of Cheapside. Remained with Mr. W. until it was time to return home.

22 MAY

Mrs. Kingcombe and George to dinner. Mrs. K. promises a reward of a handsome book to the best translator of *Delectus* at Christmas, George and myself. My Mother went to see our poor mangling woman Mrs. Bailey who broke a blood vessel some time ago.

23 MAY

To school as usual, old Monk drinks like a fish.

24 MAY

To Ave Maria Lane in the afternoon for some Plays purchased by Josiah Wright for me. Mr. and Mrs. Mitchell and their son, who resembles a bear very much, came in the evening.

25 MAY

Had something the matter with my throat in the morning which prevented my speaking and almost breathing, a similar attack which I experienced when with my Mother at Margate.

26 MAY

To my Father in the morning. Mr. Kingcombe came there in the evening. My Uncle John Pocock met with a sad accident in the Regent's Park this morning, the pole of a carriage having run against the horse he was riding, he took fright and threw my Uncle off with great violence and broke four of his ribs.

27 MAY, Sunday

Went to Paddington Church with Emily, Eliza, Tom and Lew in the morning. Mr. and Mrs. Kingcombe came to dinner, then went over our Well Cottage as they think of living in it.

28 MAY

My Mother and Emily went to town early in the morning and I to school. They called on the Underwoods, Phoebe and Emma U. and Lucy Harper [*their niece*] are preparing for Epsom races which commence on Thursday.

31 MAY

Went to the Tax Gatherer, Edgware Road, with Mr. Mitchell in the morning, thence to my Father. Lloyd there. On my return called at St. Bride's, Uncle is recovering fast.

2 JUN

Went after school to my Father where I saw Mr. and Mrs. Kingcombe. Called on my Uncle who is quite out of danger.

3 JUN

Mr. Gurney and Tom in the Morning who stayed dinner. Walked with them as far as the Yorkshire Stingo [*an ancient inn with a bowling green, which stood on what is now the Marylebone Road*] on their return at night.

4 JUN

To school, delightful warm weather.

5 Jun
Boys commencing 'vacation' letters to-day, holidays to commence.

8 Jun
To school as usual, *pen knife nut crackers* very plentiful just now, while letter writing continues.

10 Jun, Sunday
Went to Paddington Church with Eliza and Emily in the morning, at home all the afternoon.

12 Jun
To school. The boys have to *'fork out'* as they call it, one penny for every sheet of paper spoiled in letter writing.

13 Jun
To School, boys growling tremendously at the new *forking out* system. Some have lost three weeks advance Spend money.

15 Jun
Went to my Father, accompanied young Ramsden in the Banco Regis to have a game at rackets.

19 Jun
School broke up this morning, recommences 23 Jul. A Grand Gala at Hintons', Eyre Arms [*named after the Eyre family, which owned the land where it stood in St. John's Wood*], Wellington Road, saw some excellent fire works there.

22 Jun
Went to Papa early, Mr. Kingcombe there. Walked with Papa to Mr. Williams, Stock Exchange and other places in the City, took tea at St. Bride's. Uncle is at Bath.

23 Jun
Went to Peele's Coffee House in the morning, met my Father in Fetter Lane who returned with me, leaving again in the evening. Mr. Kingcombe removed from Battersea to No. 26 Stamford Street [*linking Lambeth to Southwark*].

24 Jun
A gentleman called from Mr. Abrahams, to inspect some land. Emily and Eliza only went to church.

25 JUN

Papa came home to meet Messrs. Mortimer and Shaw concerning our house.

26 JUN

Mr. Mortimer with Mr. Shaw came in the morning, the business was not, however, concluded.

27 JUN

My Mother and Papa at the Shackles' and also Mr. and Mrs. Gurney, who removed on Saturday to Highgate.

28 JUN

At home all day amusing myself with the children

29 JUN

Visited Mrs. Kingcombe in her new house with Emily and Eliza. Fred Gurney came soon after we left and also my Father.

1 JUL, Sunday

Very dull gloomy day, no visitors.

2 JUL

Roaming about the Hilly Field [*east of Kilburn*], West End Lane most of the day.

3 JUL

Walpole Eyre, Esq., came according to appointment to meet my Father who did not make his appearance.

4 JUL

To-day is the last of Term. Surveyors of Sewers came to see my Father.

8 JUL, Sunday

Aroused by a loud ringing at the bell early in the morning, and was gratified to find Josiah Wright at the gate who came to spend the day with us. After breakfast we took a lengthy but beautiful walk to Kingsbridge 7 or 8 miles distant. Frederick and Josiah stayed with me all night.

9 JUL

Arose at 5 oclk, went with Fred and Josiah to Paddington where the latter left us. Called upon Mr. Onions, Connaught Terrace, next Mr. Mortimer's, Piccadilly, where Fred and I parted. Next walked to my father, home in the eveng.

13 JUL

In the morning I trudged to Papa, remained with him until sunset and then trudged back again.

14 JUL

To my Father. Bought some fruit for to-morrow on my return.

15 JUL, Sunday

Nothing particular, no visiting to-day.

18 JUL

In the afternoon Emma Underwood, her niece Lucy. The two girls, the two boys and myself went to Hampstead Heath so famous for donkeys. We first hired a donkey-chaise, which I drove and then rode separately on saddle *hehaws*. We were highly delighted with our afternoon sport. Emma is a rare high spirited woman, Lucy is rather a pretty girl but seems to have no animation - no life or interest about her.

20 JUL

Invited by Josiah Wright to spend Sunday with him.

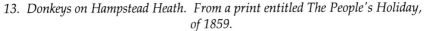

13. *Donkeys on Hampstead Heath. From a print entitled The People's Holiday, of 1859.*

22 JUL, Sunday

Walked early to Liverpool Street, Bishopsgate Street, the weather being very wet, it rained incessantly. Could not find the Wright's house. Josiah directed me to No. 1, paced the whole street through and through for two hours and more, knocked at a dozen doors, but being new comers no one knew them. Then went to my Father who told me it was No. 1 Liverpool *Buildings*, where I returned and readily found him out. Took dinner with Josiah and his father. Amused ourselves all the afternoon by looking over his collection of books and prints. He came with me as far as Tottenham Rd. p.m.

25 JUL

I was roused from sleep in the morning by a voice crying out, "Halloa Johannes, my Boy", started up and found my friend Fred Gurney by my bedside; he has come to help me fudge out some rusty old anecdotes etc. for *The Casket* [*a weekly magazine first published in February that year*]. These we transferred to writing paper in the form of two letters with the additional adornment of the Correspondent's initials. Went out together in the village after dinner, met William Robinson when we went and had a delightful bathe in a fine pond which is in a field on the bye-road to Willesdon, as you turn from the Bell Inn over the fields [*Edgware Road, Kilburn*].

26 JUL

Fred and I went together as far as Cowie and Strange, Fetter Lane, in the morning, where we parted and I went on to my Father. In returning I called at Gurneys when it rained very hard all night, preventing my return home.

27 JUL

With Fred in the morning to Charing Cross and then (solus) to Mr. Thomas Hill Mortimer, Albany. Saw Mr. M. and returned to Papa, coming home at the usual hour.

28 JUL

To Mr. Garrett with a letter from Mama. I shall return as a day scholar again in a few days.

29 JUL, Sunday

Much talk about the late alarming thunderstorms which have visited Nottingham.

30 JUL

The Misses Eliza and Charlotte Rogers came and spent the evening with us. Emma sang very well. They invited her and Mama to a party at the Doctor's on Thursday next.

31 JUL

Emma assisting Mama to make some little frock coats for Tom and Lew, which look very neat and tasteful.

2 AUG

Went to my Father – afterwards with my Mother to Dr. Rogers who gave a grand party which did not break up until 4 a.m.

3 AUG

Mama very poorly. Went up for little Anne Rogers who came with me and spent the day with us. Played at Pope Joan in the evening.

4 AUG

Mother compelled to go to town to-day. Went to Fetter Lane for *The Casket* of to-day and to Paddington with Eliza p.m.

5 AUG, Sunday

With Emma Underwood to Oxford Street when we rode in a hackney coach to Waterloo Bridge.

6 AUG

To school in the morning. All look very grave and sedate.

7 AUG

Monk kicked up a fine hullabulleroo at my Latin as my Exempla minoma exercises were imperfect, who cares for old Monkey.

8 AUG

Got to school pretty early and went through the ugly Latin a little better, what crackjaws the Romans must have had.

9 AUG

Half holiday. Mr. Monk is a regular cross old stick.

10 AUG

Obliged to go to Town as Papa wanted me. Emma left to-day taking Eliza to stay a week at Brixton. Mama had a letter from Josiah Wright inviting me and her to accompany him to his mother's who has taken a large boarding house in Caroline Place at Hastings. We cannot go.

11 AUG

Went to Josiah and saw him safe off in the Hastings mail from the Bolt [*the Bolt-in-Tun tavern*] in Fleet Street at ½ past 7 p.m.

12 AUG, Sunday

In the forenoon I went to Gurney's, remained for dinner, thereafter which Fred and I went to my Father to whom I took some of his favourite fruit from our garden, namely russet pippins.

[*The name of this recalls the most distressing recollections to my mind, it was a russet which my father gave me the Sunday subsequent [sic] to his decease when, with tears in his eyes he bid us all a last and long farewell. This apple I have still in my box although it has become like he who gave it to me, withered, sapless, shrunk, dead!* John Pocock, 1835]

13 AUG

Went to school, rattling on in Phiedrus Fables.

16 AUG

To school in the morning. It is very strange we do not hear from George for we know not as yet whether James arrived safe on the Island.

17 AUG

To Hacker's, Hadlow Street, Burton Crescent, early in the morning for an amount due to Papa. I then went through Frith Street to Capt. Murray.

18 AUG

To school. Much talk about Mr. Canning's death. [*George Canning (1770-1827), Prime Minister died 8 August.*]

20 AUG

To school very late as my Mother came with me on the road to Town. Monk boxed my ears and shook me so unmercifully that he shook all the Latin out of my noddle at the same time.

22 AUG

To School as usual, all right with Mr Phedrus.

23 AUG

Mr. Garrett invited me to a gipsy hunting party as he called it. He hired the Lord's Cricket Ground [*Thomas Lord had opened his St. John's Wood cricket ground in 1814*] for the day upon which we played at that healthy game, I got only 8 runs coming in, the last innings, our side lost the day. Found a gentleman at our house on my return who came about some furniture.

24 AUG

Removed some of the drawing room furniture to Suffolk St., Southwark, Papa

14. Lord's cricket ground in 1837. Detail from a design printed on a silk handerchief.

having parted with it. Went to Marylebone Lane where I got my plays. George and Sampson Kingcombe are ill with brain fever.

25 AUG
Went to school, afterwards to my Father. Fred Gurney is apprenticed to Gates the Chemist, Whitechapel, Mr. Gurney has removed.

27 AUG
Forgot to go to Josiah as intended, after school hours.

28 AUG
To School. One Lardner there the son of a poor Irish clergyman will I think turn out a clever fellow, he learns double lessons from inclinations, a great rarity.

29 AUG
Mama, Emily and Eliza went to Haymarket Theatre with Emma Underwood and her beau. I stayed up until they came home.

1 SEP

Went to Mr. Wright's after dinner, nobody at home, then went to Papa. Lost my pretty dog near the Monument, poor fellow, I hope he will get into good hands.

3 SEP

George Kingcombe is fast recovering which I am glad to hear.

6 SEP

Went to school. Have to say Delectus, Mondays and Fridays, and Phoedrus Fables, Thursdays and Saturdays.

10 SEP

Went to Papa and afterwards to Brixton. All Eliza's clothes have been stolen with many others belonging to the family.

12 SEP

To School as usual, Old Monk is a queer one indeed.

13 SEP

To School in pretty good time for a wonder.

14 SEP

Old Monk very cross to-day. He boxed my ears and gave me 10 lines as a task. I should have been kept and had the consolation of seeing all the boys eat a hearty dinner with an empty stomach, had it not been for Mr. Smiden the under Latin teacher, who got me off.

15 SEP

I walked to Paddington after tea for my periodicals.

16 SEP

Children went to church. I went with Robinson to his Uncle's to see some very curious monkeys, such as were never brought into England before. William's mother gave us some fine nectarines.

17 SEP

Mother went to Town when I set off for school. Called on Mr. Wright who went with me to Kingcombe's for the purpose of seeing Mama. Spent a pleasant evening, played at Speculations and returned with Mama at night.

18 SEP

While at school a letter came from George to Bilney and at home one for Papa, Mama, Mr. Kingcombe and myself. Also one for Papa from James Magson who had safely arrived at St. Helena. George is persuading Papa to let me go out to China in the Compy. service as a midshipman. I should like nothing better.

19 SEP

Took Mr. Garrett George's letters to read. After school went to Kingcombes' and then Papa, who says he will think about me becoming a *middy*, I can think about nothing else.

21 SEP

Mama sent Emily to school with some sandwiches for me, she took my books home, when I went to Spitalfields on business for James Magson. Returned at 8 oclk P.M.

23 SEP, Sunday

Edward Kingcombe has fallen down an area in Southampton Street which has plunged his poor mother in greater grief than ever.

28 SEP

Fred Gurney's birthday. Went to the Angel and Crown after school and met him there. We spent a jovial evening with his Papa and brothers.

29 SEP

Michaelmas Day, nothing but geese alive and dead at all corners to be met with.

30 SEP, Sunday

Mr. Noyes called in the evening and had a chat with us about George; Noyes is a sensible plain plodding man. Covent Garden, Drury Theatres open to-morrow evening. Kean comes at Covent Garden and his son [*Charles Kean (1811-68) appeared at Drury Lane in 1827 as 'Young Norval'*] at Old Drury, his first appearance.

2 OCT

To School in the morning. I have an excellent character from Mr. G. who sets me forth as a pattern to the other boys, but I would much rather be a great rascal and a good scholar like many of them instead of being 'old steady' only.

3 OCT

Went to school as usual, everything passing *riglar*.

4 OCT

Eliza met me in St. John's Wood Road and took my books home while I went on to my Father.

5 OCT

Went to school and came home the fields way.

7 OCT, Sunday

Robinson the bricklayer found his way into Marylebone Watch House being *so-so* last night.

9 OCT

To School which is increasing very much. We have now a matter of 68 boarders and about 15 day pupils.

10 OCT

To School, dull dreary School, as usual.

11 OCT

Mama went to the City and I set out to escort her home in the evening, met her upon Maida Hill.

13 OCT

Received £30 from the Metropolitan Road Committee, went to my Father and returned home with Mama.

14 OCT, Sunday

My Mother with Emily and Eliza went to take dinner with my father in town, William Robinson came and spent the day with me. I succeeded in pursuading him to keep a journal.

18 OCT

My Mother called to see Mrs. Wright. Saw the following advertisement in the *Times* of Monday under the head of Marriages –

 'At St. Bartolph [St Botolph] Bishopsgate Mr Brown of Cheapside to Miss Caroline Wright of Hastings.'

19 OCT

Went to School, note Friday, it is always my unlucky day!

20 OCT

Walked to Spital Fields, then to my Father had tea with my Uncle John.

22 OCT

Went to School. I observe that Mr. G. is always more strict upon a Monday than any other day and talks about *turning over a new leaf* more.

24 OCT

Had the spasms very bad, very bad in the morning, which prevented me going to school.

25 OCT

Went to school as usual, some queer remarks about spasms from Mr. Garrett.

26 OCT

Cricked my neck in the morning, did not go to school. Went with Emily to a Mr. Pullen, Lisson Grove. We called upon our kind old servant Elizth. Stone, who is living with Mr. Clark, Medina Place, on our way home.

27 OCT

My neck very painful, went to a doctor in Paddington who gave me something for it. Papa came home at night rather unwell.

28 OCT, Sunday

Raining the whole day. Papa very unwell complaining of a pain in the back.

1 NOV

Mrs Yates [*washerwoman*] working all day, she is very fond of gin.

6 NOV

To school as usual. Mr. Monk has gone, on the old score I suppose.

7 NOV

Went to Mr. Underwood to dinner and then to the Borough for some papers. Could not make anyone hear the bell on my return nor could I see any light. Rang for half an hour then went to Robinson, called him up and he came down with Jay. After a great deal of ringing the girl came, she had fallen asleep and the candle did the same. Mother and Father came home soon after. William slept with me.

8 NOV

Papa went to the Albany in the morning. Mr. Mortimer is out of town. My Father returned at night.

9 NOV

Lord Mayor's Day. The two girls and boys went to Uncle's to see the Show. I remained at home. Mama left Tom and Lew at Kingcombes'.

10 NOV

Fetched my brothers from Mr. Kingcombe. Carried Lew great part of the way, he being too fat to walk so long a distance. [*John's brother Lewis was then aged four; the distance from Stamford Street to Kilburn is about eight miles.*]

12 NOV

My Father walked with me as far as St. John's Wood Chapel in the morning on his road to town, remained all night.

13 NOV

Went to Paddington after school to have my wig cropped.

14 NOV

A new Latin and French master came this morning in place of Monk, of the name of Fleming.

15 NOV

To Paddington after school to get some medicine for Maria, doctors are very dear.

16 NOV

Mrs Garrett gave me a cocoa nut which came from her brother in Jamaica.

18 NOV

Tott [*family servant*] called in the morning, he seems very ill.

22 NOV

Went over the fields with Papa, first to Russell's, then to Abraham's, Russell Square, next to Gurney's where we parted. I then went to Mrs. Coleford in the Borough and met Papa again at Shackle's, Percival Street [*Finsbury*]. We saw Mrs. Bean [*sister-in-law of John's uncle John Pocock*] there, and then attended a sale at the Auction Mart by Williams who had wine and books principally for sale. Then again to Gurney's, had a game at cards with Tom and May and walked home with Papa at 8 oclk; very frosty night.

24 NOV

Eliza Kingcombe is dangerously ill of brain fever.

26 NOV

Went to the Court House, Marylebone, with my Father in the morning, then to Mr. Brown, Wells Street. Afterwards to Gurney's when Papa sent me to Hampstead. I lost my way, having taken the Highgate Road instead, was almost in the mud and had to make the best of my way home without completing my journey.

29 Nov

Did not go to School, went to Mr. Cocker's for my Father. Dined at Gurneys, and met our school out walking on my return home.

1 Dec

Emily's birthday, did not go to school. Attempted to fly George's kite but did not succeed.

2 Dec, Sunday

Papa went early to Hampstead and then to Gurneys' where my Mother and Emily met him. Robinson came in the afternoon and accompanied me to Gurneys', we were nicely soaked with rain. Saw Fred at home. We all returned in the evening.

4 Dec

To School. Mrs. Garrett requested me to make enquiries about a servt. she had hired, which I was about to do but she came. Papa returned in the evening, having slept with Mr. Kingcombe last night.

11 Dec

To school, which was rather in confusion. Break up tomorrow.

12 Dec

I think it very curious that we should break up on my birthday, especially as this will probably be the last day of my going to school. I am now 13 years of age and am about to enter the world, as Papa intends I should go into business soon.

15 Dec

Went to Paddington to get *The Casket* etc., saw William Robinson in the evening and had a game at all fours with him. My Father came from Walham Green.

19 Dec

Let the little cottage to-day for £20-10-0d per ann. to Arnold – who has possession on Christmas Eve. Went to my Uncle and got wet through in coming home.

21 Dec

With my Father to Gurneys', where I remained until evening. Papa went to his Attorneys, Messrs. Robinson and Hines in Charter House Square.

22 Dec

Papa went to Gurneys' in the morning. Tott called whom we sent there after Papa, after which I also went there and accompanied my Father to Robinson & Hines to receive some money.

23 DEC, Sunday

My friend Josiah Wright came to see us in the afternoon. He, with Papa and myself went to Robinsons', invited Robinson for Christmas Day.

24 DEC

At home all day. Mrs. Kingcombe invited all the family to her home to-morrow, I shall, however, remain at home.

25 DEC

My Father, Mother, and all the children went to Mr. Kingcombe where they dined and spent the day. Self and Robinson remained at Kilburn, were rather dull by ourselves, went to bed early.

26 DEC

Mama and the children came home to tea, Papa soon after. They were very happy yesterday at the Kingcombes'.

28 DEC

Mrs. Gates the washerwoman washing all day. Papa came home in the afternoon. Mama is still at Underwoods'.

29 DEC

Mama returned from Brixton in the evening. Lucy Harper is to go to Colchester shortly for 3 years to a Boarding School and we youngsters are invited to a party at Mrs. Miller's previous to her departure.

31 DEC

Went to Mrs. King whose foreman Everest measured me for a suit of clothes, after which we called at Kingcombe's. Mrs. K. is very ill, then called upon my Uncle. Mrs Bartlett, her two daughters and Betsy [*Isabella Bartlett was John's aunt and his uncle John's sister, the widow of Thomas Bartlett, attorney, by whom she had two daughters, Martha and Mary Ann, Betsy being the latter's nineteen-year-old daughter*] were there to celebrate my Uncle's birthday, took tea with them and we called lastly at Gurneys', saw Tom who happened to be at home. We bought a few figs to keep our teeth from freezing together and stopped a short time at Lyon Terrace hearing a band playing very well, then walked home without any further adventures.

Chapter Three

At Work

1 JAN, 1828
All our family at home, it being a very dull wet day. Mama sorted the large draw full of her letters in the evening.

3 JAN
With Papa to Russells and the Regents Park early, then to Gurneys, and directly thereafter to Westons. I went to F. Williams, Stock Exchange, with a letter, Josiah overtook me on Ludgate Hill. Returned to Gurneys and after tea came home with my Father.

4 JAN
My Father went to London in the morning and I followed. Fetched the plan home which was left at Gurneys. Bought *The Casket* at the publishers in Fetter Lane.

6 JAN, Sunday
Tott called in the morning, poor fellow he is very ill. Mama made him some nice soup for lunch, he wishes Papa had work for him again. My Father, Emily and self commenced writing letters to George after tea.

7 JAN
Mr. Kingcombe called and took tea with us. I was invited to a party but could not go as the rascally tailor has not finished my clothes.

8 JAN
Left home with my Father at 7 oclk in the morning. Walked to Vauxhall Bridge and were then rowed across the Thames to the Palace [*the horse-ferry crossed the Thames at the bottom of the modern Horseferry Road*]. We then went to Robinson's, Michell's etc., after dinner we returned home in a cabriolet from the Westminster Bridge.

9 JAN
Mr. Kingcombe came to dinner, walked to Hayward's in the evening to fetch a gun which Papa bought for me, it is however out of repair. Met Mr. K. at Pineapple Gate going home.

10 JAN

Mr. Garrett has lost a lawsuit at Guildhall with the French rascal who hit me such a crack on the head with Mr. G.'s cane during his absence one night. The cause stood thus, De Cressa v. Garrett, judgment for the plaintiff.

11 JAN

I went to King's with Tom Gurney for my new clothes, a dashing dark green suit, surtout etc., a-hem! Found Mama at Kingcombes and we came home part of the way in a Hackney coach. Saw Jack Arnold the pig killer reeling home in the 'sun' as they say.

13 JAN, Sunday

William Robinson came to tea – and I went afterwards with him to Chapel. William is very religious which is more than I can say of myself.

17 JAN

Rode in Baldwin's chaise with my father to town in the morning, & after dinner returned home, immediately after tea set off for Gurney's, who have a party to-night, expected Papa but he did not come & Mrs. G. persuaded me to stay all night which I did.

18 JAN

Out with Tom Gurney in the morning who walked with me as far as Hyde Park on my way home in the afternoon.

19 JAN

Saw one of Gurney's new Steam carriages [*this was designed by Sir Goldsworthy Gurney (1793-1875), seated fourteen and was capable of 15 m.p.h.*] running up the Edgeware Road in style.

21 JAN

Mama & Emily went to Oxford Street to make a few purchases.

22 JAN

Went to Mrs. Kingcombe, who is too ill to attend our party tomorrow, secured George by bringing him home with me, called on Gurneys who will not disappoint us.

23 JAN

William Robinson & Anne Rogers arrived at ½ past 2, soon after Mr. Kingcombe & the children, then Papa with Mrs Carter of Walham Green. Thomas, Fred & Mary Gurney came early in the evening, then the fiddlers & lastly Charlotte &

15. Gurney's Steam Carriage, which the diarist saw 'running up Edgeware Road in style'; a lithograph of 1827 by George Scharf.

Eliza Rogers and Josiah Wright, when we commenced dancing, Mary Gurney & Miss Carter were alternately my partners, Fred seemed so jealous of little Anne Rogers that I could not dance with her the whole evening, Mary Gurney is a very pretty elegant girl but am fearful she is rather proud, she is an excellent dancer, I mortified her a little by paying very great attention to Miss Carter whom I discovered was undeservedly neglected. After dancing & supper we had many good songs, but sadly missed the Underwoods & Harpers as well as Miss Hall and Mr. Gosling who sadly disappointed us. At 3 oclk Miss Rogers, Josiah Wright & W. Robinson returned home & we accommodated all the remainder with beds having spent a very pleasant night. Papa was particularly in high spirits & amused us youngsters very much with his One, Two, Three, Hop, Jog.

24 JAN
Mr. Kingcombe took all his young fry home save Eliza who remained, had fine fun with our remaining visitors.

25 JAN
In the morning I walked as far as the end of Park Road with Tom Gurney & called at Mr. Garrett's on my return. Mrs. G. was very friendly & seemed glad to see me, amused myself with the young ladies on coming home.

26 JAN

Went with Miss Carter across Hyde Park in the morning & saw her safely deposited in a Fulham Stage, then purchased my periodicals & came home. Papa returned later.

27 JAN, Sunday

Took a pleasant walk in the afternoon with Mary Gurney & my two sisters, saw Robinson in the village who went with us past Cricklewood House [*which stood at the corner of Edgware Road and the modern Cricklewood Lane*]. Went to chapel in the evening.

29 JAN

With my Father to Carter's in the morning, & then went to Robinsons in Southwark for him and met again at St. Bride's [*Wharf*] where we saw Uncle [*J.T.P. Senior*] called at Back Hill & Gurneys on our road home.

30 JAN

In the morning with my Father to Paddington where he took stage to Islington, I went to Gloster Coffee House, Oxford Street, for the purpose of meeting Walmsley, who did not appear, met my Father at Gurneys, called with him on Mortimer & Cocker & then went to Walham Green, Papa left me at Carters all night and as he & his daughter were to spend the evening at Fulham I accompanied them to their friends there, it was quite dark when we arrived but I saw enough of the town to prepossess me strongly in its favour. I always loved anything ancient, & its old queer-fashioned mansions with the irregular gables jutting into the street made me regret leaving the place without seeing more of it, we returned abut 10 oclk.

31 JAN

Walked over the large garden & orchards with Miss Carter in the morning & then went with her & her father to Carters in Bear Street (He is a native of St. Helena) where we met my father by appointment & I went home with him & called on Mr. Oldfield in our road, then oxtail soup in Bear Street.

2 FEB

To Mr. Oldfield's new buildings in the morning with my Father, after which I went with my Mother to Mr Shackles where my father met us in the evening. I then went to Mrs. Wright & remained all night, played at cribbage with Josiah & his father whom I beat but Josse beat me.

3 FEB

From after breakfast, Josiah & I took a walk & passing Shoreditch Church (where my two poor sisters are buried who died in one day of hooping cough shortly before my birth) we took the Tottenham Road and reached Lower Edmonton before we turned homewards, here near the Cross, Josiah went to school, the only part of the road which took my fancy was Stamford Hill which is very picturesque. I remember having been here once before with my brother George though some years since, the road however is interesting from the circumstance of its being Johnny Gilpin's equestrian adventure which the poet Cowper has immortalised in verse. We came home to dinner very tired having walked 18 miles, spent a pleasant afternoon with Josiah among his books, he walked with me as far as the Diorama [*this forerunner of the modern cinema could seat two hundred in its auditorium at 9-10 Park Square East, Regent's Park, where they could watch changing scenes contrived by elaborate lighting and mechanical effects*].

4 FEB
To town in the morning with my Father & Mr. Young, called on Williams, the auctioneer, and Williams, the Stockbroker, Dr. & Mrs Rogers spent the evening with my parents playing whist.

5 FEB
Left home in the morning & called on Mr. Wright for my books got the large handsome family bible which my late grandmother set so much store by. I remember when she amused me during my dangerous sickness at Hackney, how carefully she treated this book wrapped in a green baize cover & one afternoon in particular after having read it a long time she told me to be very quiet & wished to take a *nap*, the whole time she slept I silently pondered on the queer word *nap* she had made use of & which I had never heard before, I was then but 4 years old & this shows how trifles will affect the infant mind for I never hear the word *nap* mentioned without fancying my venerable dear old Grandmother & the green baize covered Bible. I had great difficulty in getting home with this sacred volume as the Kilburn Stage passed me quite full.

7 FEB
With my Father as far as Drury Lane in the morning, when I went to my Uncle, saw Betsy [*cousin*] & Mr. Murrell with him, after lunch I went with Uncle to Smithfield to meet Papa who had left. I then went to the Mansion House Inn but could not find him, after which I called at Gurneys', waited for him until 9 oclk, & then went home where he had arrived before me.

8 FEB
Sister Eliza's birthday, went to Paddington with Papa & Mr. Jay and then across the fields to Walmesleys' where we dined & returned in the evening.

9 FEB

Papa called at the Fleet Prison, or No. 9 as it is called, to see old Mr. Mansfield who is confined for a debt, called also on Gurneys returning home.

10 FEB

An officer named Bushnell who was rather lame from a wound received in the battle of Waterloo spent the afternoon with us & returned after tea, he amused us with many anecdotes connected with that glorious battle.

12 FEB

With my father to town who is trying to effect a settlement with Mortimer.

14 FEB

Uncle came in the morning. I went to the Old Ship, Customs House, to meet my Father who did not come. Papa is thinking of getting me into the Custom House with a Mr. Jennings whom we were to have seen at the Old Ship.

16 FEB

To my Uncle's in the morning who was not at home, then to Mr. Kingcombe, with him I went to the Old Ship & met Papa there, called on Uncle on our return.

19 FEB

Lew's birthday, met my father & Mr. Jennings at the Custom House. I do not think we shall conclude with him.

22 FEB

To St. Bride's in the morning, had a long conversation with Lewis about George & took a letter for him to the East India House.

23 FEB

My father went to Mr. Mortimer & remained five hours with him arranging accounts, Mr. M. is to write to Col. Howard on Monday concerning the allowance to be made my Father [*for*] his Guardianship of the Greville Hill estate [*this had been jointly owned by George Pocock, Thomas Mortimer, the Hon. Fulke Greville Howard and Daniel Chapman*].

24 FEB

Mr. Bennett from Westminster came in the morning, I walked with him as far as Ennes' Mill before dinner. Mr. Carew, the statuary [*John Carew (1785-1868) was currently employed at Petworth*], called in the afternoon.

25 FEB

My mother treated me to Covent Garden Theatre, went with her & saw *Richard IIIrd* & *The Somnabulist*. I was much delighted as Kean played Gloster very well, *The Somnabulist* is a very pretty piece.

26 FEB

Went in the morning with my Father to the new St. Catherine's Dock now in course of erection [*St Katharine's Dock was to be opened the following October*], dined with Uncle, Samuel [*Samuel Pocock, then aged twenty-four, was the eldest son of John's uncle, John Pocock*] is very ill. Called on Gurneys in the evening. Mrs. G. told us her brother George Edward had been found drowned in the City Canal & had been three weeks in the water when discovered.

28 FEB

Walked up to Dr. Rogers with my Father in the morning, the three children, Eliza, Tom and Lew will go to Miss Rogers school on Monday.

29 FEB

Papa went to town in the morning & arranged with Mr. Cocker for me to attend in his office as a junior clerk. Made a little garden for myself at the top of my Father's close to the peach trees.

1 MAR

My Mother went to Town & returned with Papa in the evening having met him at Gurney's. I went to Paddington in the evening & met Robinson on the road, Uncle and Samuel came in the evening & lodged at the Bell Inn.

2 MAR, Sunday

Walked about the village & fields all the morning with Uncle and Papa then went to Holloway with them & Jay, we went over the new Caledonian Asylum [*an orphanage for Scottish children founded in what is now the Caledonian Road in 1815*] which is built on part of my Uncle's estate, then came home.

3 MAR

My dear Mother's birthday, walked with Josiah who came home with Emily last night as far as the Stingo & then went on to the office with Papa in Nassau Street, Soho. I felt very timid at first & was given a long letter to copy for a Mr. Evan Evans in Wales, there are two clerks Messrs. Stevens and Whittaker besides Mr. Barker who is almost a partner to Mr. Cocker. Went to the Stamp Office and Throgmorten Street with Whittaker.

16. The new Caledonian Asylum for Scottish orphans was erected in what became the Caledonian Road, Islington in 1828, on one of the Pocock estates.

4 MAR

To office early in the morning where I was engaged copying a deed. Went to Bridge Street, Blackfriars & met Uncle in Drury Lane who asked me concerning my situation, returned at 5 p.m. my Father gone to Walmesley. Won the vast sum of *one penny* from Mama at cribbage in the evening.

5 MAR

In the office copying a deed all day, Mother went to Brixton.

6 MAR

Went to Stamp Office, Somerset House, to get some indentures stamped. Mrs. Rogers to tea & a rubber of whist.

7 MAR

My hours of attendance at Cocker's are from 10 a.m. until 5 p.m. *The Casket* came out to-day with good view of the late Brunswick Theatre now a heap of ruins. [*Opened in Well Street at the end of February it had collapsed three days later during a rehearsal, because of the weight of its roof, killing twelve.*]

8 MAR

Clerks gave me the name of 'Jack the Green' from my dashing green surtout, a plague on their impudence.

9 MAR, Sunday

Mrs. Wolff (wife of the Indian bashaw) came to show Mama her troop of children who are very fine considering they are such ferocious animals.

10 MAR

To the office early. I have a long indenture to copy all about 'a simple pew in a certain Church aforesaid', etc.

11 MAR

To the office all day writing about 'the pew aforesaid'.

12 MAR

Father called at the office and took me out to lunch with him. I went to Uncle's with him & afterwards met my Mother in St. Paul's Churchyard with whom I came home.

13 MAR

In the Stamp Office in the course of the day, home at 6 p.m.

15 MAR

Went to Mr. Bethell Chancery Lane. He is the Counsel in a Chancery suit in which *we* are solicitors (Hum!).

16 MAR, Sunday

Tott called in the morning to ask my Father's advice concerning a watch which he had found & sold. Mama & self trotted off to Carter's, Walham Green, where we dined & spent the afternoon. Papa walked as far as Tyburn Gate with us.

19 MAR

In the office as usual, came home at 5 o'clk *quite ready* for dinner although dinner was not *quite ready* for me.

20 MAR

Papa met Mr. Carew at Mortimer's to arrange some business between them, I am almost tired of the 'pew aforesaid', it occupies nearly four quires of foolscap.

21 MAR

To the Stamp Office. Young Walmsley called at Cocker's & seemed to have the stomach ache at seeing me there, I began whistling by way of a cure for he sadly wished to get in the office. Rode home from Paddington with Mr. Carew in his phaeton.

22 MAR

Wrote to Josiah Wright requesting him to meet me at Hampstead Church tomorrow morning. Mr. Barker gave me a copy of writ to serve on a man residing in Bury Street, Fulham Road, but it would not do. 'Not at Home - quite uncertain when he will be in' which proved a dead hit.

23 MAR, Sunday

Walked to Carter's (with dog) early in the morning, found him preparing to come to our house in his chaise cart, poked dog in behind, seated myself by Miss Carter when the old gent put his whip to use & we started for Kilbourne, but did not arrive until dinner time as Mr. C. made so many calls on the road.

Found Josiah there. Phoebe Underwood was convulsed with laughter as Mr. Carter repeated declaration of his liking to "no form, ceremonies". Miss C. returned with her father which is not 'according to contract'.

25 MAR

Came home at the usual time, Papa dined with me & afterwards attended Pope Joan party at the doctor's, went there to speak to Mama and played ½ an hour.

27 MAR

Papa called at the office in the morning & told me Miss U. and my Mother were going to Covent Garden Theatre to see *Othello*. Met them by Tyburn Turnpike, walked with Papa to Mr. Wolff in the afternoon & with him to Oxford Street to meet the ladies for whom we had the satisfaction of waiting in the cold bleak wind just three quarters of an hour, don't like such tragedies as these, can see no *play* in them.

31 MAR

Mama went to town in the morning with a gentleman from my Father. I rode with them in a hackney coach to Regent Street.

1 APR

My Mother and Father came home in the afternoon having settled Bewley's claim with the assistance of Mr. Holmes.

2 APR

Had my hair cut most shamefully by a rascally Paddington barber. Mrs. Underwood who was at our home followed the *whig's* example by *taking off* my hair when I came home.

4 APR

Good Friday a holiday at the office, took a delightful rural walk almost as far as Edgware. Oh how I love the Country! Dr. Rogers gave me a ride in his gig coming back.

5 APR

Josiah Wright called in the morning & invited me to his house, went accordingly from the office there, had tea & played cribbage with him & another gentleman.

6 APR, Sunday

Left Smoke & London with Josiah in the morning for a long walk. We took the Whitechapel road & went first to Bow with its Church. I was very much pleased because of its antiquity. We then took a circuitous route to Hadley, here we had a pleasant view with the telescope, the church is a very fine old structure & we passed through the yard. Oh how delightful is it to ponder on the gravestones those who were snuffed off in their youth & blossom, how useful a lesson to the living, Josiah is not so gloomy as me, he passed them with a mere observation, but I could linger for hours there. We then went on to Bromley in Kent, thence to Beckenham & lastly Stepney then home, we enjoyed our walk very much. It must have been easily thirty miles. Josiah like myself is a rare pedestrian.

7 APR

Very wet & dull morning, walked with Josiah to Ludgate Hill on my way to office, got comfortably wet through on the road.

17. Hadley church.

9 APR

Holiday at the office. Went to the British Museum with my Father to show a gentleman there the Roman Coins I have to sell for Stevens and then to my Uncle who purchased them for 15/- when he heard I should have a good commission. Came home after tea.

10 APR

Took 3 volumes of my *British Theatre* and 1 of *The Casket* to the binders in the morning. Came home at the usual time.

12 APR

To the office as usual, Mr. Cocker is absent in the country courting.

13 APR

Went to West End Chapel in the morning with Robinson, Emily, Tom & Lew, in the afternoon took a walk to Mill Hill with William, Mrs. Wolff, & a whole posse of youngsters came in the afternoon, really these are a fine sample of superior bred *wolves*.

14 APR

A Mr. and Mrs. Westall called in the morning & think of taking part of our house which is so much too large even for our large family.

16 APR

My Father agreed with Mr. Westall who comes on Monday. My Mother went to Kingcombe's.

18 APR

To the office as usual. Mr. C. is still out of town & I have finished the *long brief*.

19 APR

Got my books in the morning at Paddington, Whittaker much amused with them.

20 APR

To Hampstead Church in the morning with Robinson, Emily, Tom & Lew went to St. John's Wood Chapel, & Mama & Eliza to Paddington Church in the evening.

21 APR

Mr. Westall removed into our house to-day, they have two bedrooms, the long parlour and one of the four front rooms on the ground storey.

22 APR

Mr Cocker returned to-day & I was very busy all day in consequence.

23 APR

To Bond Street with Robinson in the evening to see the illuminations & got wet through in the passage.

24 APR

My brother George's birthday. His Majesty held a splendid levee at St. James Palace, yesterday which was thronged with the flowers of nobility. The Duchess of St. Albans (Mrs. Coates) [*the former actress, Mrs Harriot Coutts - widow of the banker and known in the theatre as Harriot Mellon - had married the Duke of St. Albans in 1827*] was present.

25 APR

To Gray's Inn for Mr. Cocker. Writing most part of the day.

26 APR

As my Mother & Father & self were leaving for Underwoods', Mr. Carter & son of Bear Street arrived in a cabriolet. Young C. politely handed my Mother in his place who rode to town & we again met them then continued our route to Brixton. After dinner Mama & self with the two girls went to see Mrs. Gurney. Capt. G. is very ill with his *old friend* the *gout*. Tom G. came back with the Underwoods and Mr. U. & Phoebe walked with us as far as Vauxhall Bridge, on our way home we called on Mrs. Wilson who pressed us to stop but it was then too late.

28 APR

To Gray's Inn for Mr. C. met Mrs. Brown & a young lady at the top of Drury Lane. Mr. Underwood took tea with us, saw Robinson in the evening who tells me he spent yesterday very pleasantly with Josiah Wright at Highgate.

29 APR

Called for my books coming home which are well bound, met Robinson in Paddington who came home with me. Mrs. Gurney invited all our youngsters to her house on Sunday next.

1 MAY

Chimney sweepers day, plenty of *Jacks* in the *Green* [*May Day revellers dressed in leaves*] like myself....

2 MAY

Sweepers drumming all over town again to-day.

3 MAY

Had to run as fast as I could to the Stamp Office, arrived there four minutes before they closed, made out my warrant in one minute, boxed it in two more & answered to claim with the last just in time.

6 MAY
Robinson obtained a situation with Green the Auctioneer of Davies Street, Oxford Street by interest of his Uncle.

8 MAY
My Father called in the morning & consulted with Mr. C. about allowing me a salary but I fear he (Mr. C.) is too stingy!

10 MAY
To Bridge St., Blackfriars, called at St. Bride's, saw Samuel. Robinson overtook me at Pine Apple Gate. Papa & Mr. Westall played draughts together in the evening. Papa told him I was the greatest screw [*miser*] in the world & Mama drank as a treat "Frugality without meanness", hard rules for me & I may add unmerited ones.

11 MAY
The two girls went to Marylebone Church in the morning.

12 MAY
The two Miss Rogers & brother James spent the evening with us & we had some good songs from them, they were very merry & happy & parted with us rather late at night.

13 MAY
My Mother & Miss Underwood came to the office per appointment when I treated them & myself to the Royal Exhibition, Somerset House [*the Royal Academy of Arts had assembled at Somerset House since 1771*]. We were much amused with the paintings but we all considered there were too many portraits, *Drunkard* is very good & the *Spectacles* and *Disappointed Swain* in particular are excellent, the latter represents a jolly Jack Tar going into church with his bride & a disappointed Soldier sitting close by looking most indescribably as if he could not help it. We were four hours in the rooms & did not examine half the paintings so numerous were they.

16 MAY
Went to the Vice-Chancellor's Court held at Westminster. His Honour did not hear our cause, then to the Counsel Bethell with briefs etc., went to Underwoods' from office & remained the night.

17 MAY

Left Brixton at 9 oclk & got to the office at the usual hour. Papa called soon after, went on to Court at Westminster, saw our counsel, the trial to come on by consent on Thursday. Stuart our Scotch neighbour grossly insulting Father, I wish I was a little bigger to give him a good hiding.

18 MAY, Sunday

Tom & Mary Gurney arrived at 10 oclk and Fred soon after. Robinson came soon after dinner & we boys went to the Bell Tea Gardens [*behind the Bell Inn, Kilburn*] where we took some cyder.

19 MAY

To Mr Starbridge, Tottenham Court Road and Bethell's Chambers in the afternoon, also to Lombard Street for the office copy answer [*copied documents*]. Delighted Tom & Lew by riding them in a wheelbarrow on my return. Robinson played Speculation [*a card game*] with me in the evening.

21 MAY

To Somerset House for Stamps, my warrant exceeded £40.

24 MAY

Emily went to Paddington with me in the morning, a soldier's funeral overtook me in Park Lane, it was one of that fine cavalry regiment quartered in Knightsbridge and never was I more gratified than with the great respect shown the deceased. First came a few soldiers with their firelocks pointing to the earth, then the corpse born by his comrades, the polished helmet at the head of the black covered coffin. Methought the fine raven plume of feathers waved mournfully with the breeze, at the front were a fine pair of horse pistols, then came his followers, & the band playing a mournful air, & lastly what pleased us most was his splendid black charger with his master's boots & sword buckled on. Himself too ready accoutred, ah, all was as usual save the man; instinctively I followed them all the way to St. George's, Hanover Square, where after the usual beautiful service a volley was fired over his grave; this chapel is so constructed to allow the horse to pass through that he may attend his late owner to the verge of the grave. Oh, how I love to ponder upon Death!

25 MAY, Sunday

Josiah came at ½ past 10 when with me & Robinson he walked to Edgware, this is a very pretty old town, had lunch at an Inn there & returned. Josiah walked so fast I could not keep up with them & arrived ½ an hour after they came home, to the Yorkshire Stingo with him & William [*Robinson*] when he got in a Stage Coach and rode home.

26 MAY

Left home early with Emily & Eliza to go to Mr. Kingcombe's. Papa in chaise with Mr. Peters overtook & drove us to Pall Mall, we then walked on to Great Dover Street; saw the Greenwich Fair people flocking down the road by hundreds, after a nice dinner we walked to some tea gardens a mile or so down the road where we refreshed ourselves....on our return we each sang a song and Mrs. Kingcombe, good old soul, knocked us down on the floor in singing about *The Old Cobbler*. Emily and self posted off home leaving Tom, Lew & Eliza until to-morrow. I never liked Mr. Kingcombe much, but I know him well now & care not if he knows what I think of him, he is a cross, snappish cheese.

27 MAY

Very sore throat all day. My Father called for me at the office and I went home in the evening. Robinson & I walked to Hinton's [*the Eyre Arms*] where we saw some excellent fireworks, met Father & Mother at the Priory who were very angry at my going.

28 MAY

Stuart acknowledged his late ill conduct and my Father, bless him, is so very good tempered, he freely forgave him. Papa rather unwell.

29 MAY

King Charles Day, St. James gun fired 42 times.

30 MAY

To the Stamp Office, Throgmorton Street, and Old Jewry in the morning.

3 JUN

To Bethell's in the morning to take the deeds to Vice-Chancellor's Court, also to Lincolns Inn for Mr. B. While hearing the pleading my cousin Tom, the solicitor, came in, and my two late school fellows, the Thwaits with their sister, they are wards of Chancery and came to present themselves to his Honour, also Tom Gurney who has become like myself 'A limb of the Law', he is with Mr. Sandys at a good salary.

4 JUN

To Bethells and the Vice Chancellor's Court a.m. Miss Rogers came in the evening and played drafts with my Father, I saw her safe home after supper.

5 JUN

Mr. Good the noted well-digger called away Father, to office a.m.

8 JUN, Sunday

The Tailor brought home my new clothes in the morning & I stuffed his blue bag full of cabbages out of our garden, tailors are very fond of cabbage [*cabbage, or cabbaging: dishonest practice of tailors in pilfering cloth*]. The fellow took the joke and the cabbage very well. Emily went to St. John's Wood Chapel.

10 JUN

My Father has decided I shall leave Mr. Cocker this week as he will allow no salary to the Junior Clerk, my Father thinks and I agree with him that it is very discouraging to work for nothing. Dined with my Uncle who asked his usual good tempered question, "Well Mr. John, how goes the Law?"

11 JUN

Rode in the chaise with Mr. Peters and my Father to Charing Cross to Bouverie Street & the Stamp Office, met Josiah Wright under Temple Bar.

13 JUN

To Bethell's in the morning & to Fetter Lane. Cowie & Strange are publishing a new periodical *Youth Sports & Pastimes*.

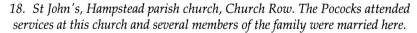

18. St John's, Hampstead parish church, Church Row. The Pococks attended services at this church and several members of the family were married here.

15 JUN, Sunday

To Hampstead Church in the morning with Emily which being 2½ miles distant through the fields we had a delightful walk there & back. To Mr. Jay with my Father at sunset – we saw two fellows, Battey & another, fighting in the field by the bourne, wicked rascals instead of being at Church. A very delightful Summer day.

16 JUN

Went to Hammersley's [*bankers*], paid in £180. To Basinghall Street, called on Uncle & dined with him & my Father, then to Charles Hall near the New Post Office & also Shackles. Returning home we called on Mr. Brown the builder in London Street.

17 JUN

To the Stamp Office, met Cousin Lewis in the Edgware Road on horseback coming home. Mr. & Mrs. Westall [*tenants*] came & had a chat with us in the evening.

19 JUN

....My father obtained me a situation with Mr. Francis, a House Agent, at 28/- per mensum to commence with and I am to go on Monday.

20 JUN

A grand review in Hyde Park this morning by the Duke of Wellington, which I could not stay to see, to Westminster where I remained 3½ hours in Court.

21 JUN, Saturday

This day I leave Alfred Richard Cocker Esquire Solicitor of No. 11 Nassau Str.,Soho, having been four months with the said Alfred Richard Cocker of No. 11 Nassau Street, Soho, aforesaid, for which said service of four months I do not receive the value of four pence. I cannot say that I like the profession much, it is exceedingly dry, my Father's quotation from Thompson upon petty-fogging lawyers will apply very well to Cocker for although I believe there are many honorable & liberal minded men among the profession I am free to acquit Mr. Cocker from so *grevious an aspersion* to a *Lawyer's Character* in a *general* way.

> "These ensnare the wretched
> in the toils of law, fomenting discord and
> perplexing right
> An iron race".

Thompson.

Mama & Eliza went to Oxford Street to buy hats for little Tom and Lewis in the evening.

22 JUN

Read the morning service at home as it rained all the forenoon concluding with readings from the Bible in lieu of a sermon. Mama, Papa & self took a walk in the evening.

24 Jun

Mr. Francis, who lives at Kilburn, called for me in the morning and we went to business together, employed myself with learning the use of their books, which I completely understood by night.

25 JUN

To the office early, remained until 6 o'clk p.m. which is to be the usual time for my departure.

26 JUN

My Father gave me some abstracts to copy on my complaining I had not enough to do, the House Agency business I clearly see is to be perfectly understood in a week.

27 JUN

Mr. F. detained me until 9 oclk. The hat-maker from the Bow brought me a fine new hat, made to order.

29 JUN, Sunday

The two Miss Coneys with Master Hall called in the morning, they wish to open an establishment for young ladies at Kilbourne & I think will take part of our large house which will be like a wilderness when Mr. Westall has left for Wales.
The youngest, Charlotte, who is at present Governess to Mrs. Garrett is engaged to Mr. Bilney, the head teacher at our School.

30 JUN

To office as usual. I have not half enough to do. My Father is fearful I shall get into lazy habits with Francis.

Chapter Four

Back to School

1 JUL, 1828

Mr. Francis I find is a *little great man* & *small large* talker. I do not like too much of the *jaw* in any man, he is moreover a Theological disputant which is altogether out of my books. I like a man who pretends to Religion to take the scriptures as he finds them, to believe implicitly all therein contained, nor dare to murmur & point out such parts as he in his puerile fancy consider *defects* for points of discussion, the sublime truths contained in the Bible are too high, too mighty, for poor insignificant mortal man to point his finger at in ridicule, and yet Francis dares do even this. Very ill all night.

2 JUL

Too ill to go to office to-day went as far as Paddington with my Father in the morning, bought some Theatrical Characters.

4 JUL

My Father christened our house 'Felix Lodge'. The word lodge is not exactly the thing for our very large three-storied house, which is more like a castle than a 'lodge'. Miss Coney will open their School in it.

5 JUL

....Mr Francis sent me to Holborn at ½ past 7, returned home much fatigued.

7 JUL

In the office all day writing fresh placards for window.

8 JUL

To Bryanstone & Portman Squares in the morning, in the office the rest of the day.

9 JUL

Mr. Francis kept me until ½ past 9 p.m. when I walked home with him and Mr. Strutt.

11 JUL

My Father walked to town with me, he is in treaty with Mr. Chappell of Bond

Street who wishes to buy a piece of our ground in Greville Hill. [*Samuel Chappell, the music publisher and piano manufacturer, was to live in a house built on this site.*]

12 JUL

Three letters arrived from George by post this morning, one for my Father, Mother & self each, he is quite well but wishes to return.

14 JUL

My Mother called at the office on her way to Brixton, where she remained all night, how comfortless & miserable our house is without her.

16 JUL

Bathed with Robinson in our old place in the evening, water very cold.

17 JUL

To the office as usual, bathed with Robinson and Vere in the aftn. The ladies, Mrs. Kingcombe and Miss Underwood, have broken their promises as usual!

18 JUL

To the office as usual. Mr. Francis is not one of the 'pay breed' and my father has determined I shall leave him this week. Received a letter from Josiah Wright inviting self and Eliza to dinner on Sunday.

19 JUL

To the office as usual, with Robinson in the water on my return. I think bathing does me much good, for I am in very bad health and low spirits and have been since with Mr. Francis.

20 JUL, Sunday

Eliza and self went to Liverpool Street in the morning, by 'water' I may almost say, for it rained nearly the whole way. Josiah was very glad to see us and we had an excellent dinner prepared for us. He saw us safe in the stage at the Bank after tea.

21 JUL

Mr. Francis to-day for the last time. Miss Coneys have taken up their residence with us.

22 JUL

Miss Eliza Deacon Falcon Maine (Bless us what a name!) came to the Miss Coneys' school to-day.

23 JUL

With my father and Mr. Twyford to see his land at Harlesden Green in the morning, then to Willesden and up the long lane home again. Mrs. Kingcombe and 'Teddy' came just in dinner time and Mr. Rogers and sister in the evening, when Miss Coney came in and we had a famous game at Pope Joan. My father made them very happy and forwarded 'intrigue' and 'maturing' between Mr. Rogers and Miss Coney; we had also many excellent songs from James [*Rogers*] and his sister, etc.

24 JUL

Mrs Kingcombe left with the 2 o'clk stage, leaving Teddy. Mr. Hale [*neighbour*] is very ill and not expected to live.

25 JUL

Mr. Westall and family left us to-day; he is going to join a firm at Leicester. I went with him to his offices when he gave me a couple of large scriptural engravings, neatly framed.

26 JUL

Mr Hale very ill still.

27 JUL, Sunday

Mr Hale expired last night at 11 o'clk. To William Robinson in the evening. On my return Miss Eliza Rogers was just leaving, when I conducted her home.

28 JUL

My father says I am to return to Francis until he permanently fixes some situation for me, which I accordingly did. I am to have an hour every day for exercise. Returned at ½ past 7 p.m.

29 JUL

Had a delightful walk over the new bridge in Hyde Park; saw several deer and the Park Keeper had a famous haul of fish out of the river.

30 JUL

In the office all day and, what was worse, unemployed.

31 JUL

My father took me to Town with him. Went to see my uncle solus and met my father in Hatton Garden – we rode home together with the Keeper of Bone Farm.

19. *'The new bridge over the Serpentine, Hyde Park' by T.H. Shepherd, published 1827.*

1 AUG

Had another walk over the Serpentine, which place I am very fond of.

3 AUG, Sunday

Mr. Price came in the morning and stayed to dinner, W. Robinson took tea with me, Mr. P. left with the 8 o'clk stage.

4 AUG

Called on Francis but did not remain. Mr. Hall has left him also.

5 AUG

My father subpoenaed as witness against Morgan at the Insolvent Court, Portugal Street [*Carey Street*], went there with him, and took tea at Uncle's.

6 AUG

Went to our Doctor's for the purpose of 'doctoring' a favourite china dish which has been broken; a favourite with Mrs. Rogers who had seen the one I repaired at home with the 'infallible composition'. They invited me to stay for dinner.

7 AUG

Stayed at home all day, arranging my little garden.

8 AUG

My father went to Kingcombe's. Bad weather for Edgware Fair pony races.

9 AUG

Went to Mr. Kingcombe's. Saw a Mr. Ryder, a surgeon there to whom my father mentioned having a continual pain in his chest.

10 AUG Sunday

Fred Gurney & Josiah Wright came in the morning & spent the day with me. We took a walk as far as Kensal Green & returning in the lane gave a man 6d. each to ride on his three donkeys to Kilburn, we went along in fine style with the exception of poor Fred who fell in love with the asses belly when nothing could persuade him from rolling first on one side & then fairly under the creature's belly, he was not much hurt. Fred went home at 9 o'clk & I walked with him to Paddington, Josiah at 10 o'clk with whom I also went part of the way home.

11 AUG

To Paddington before breakfast, with my Father as far as Soho, when I pursued my way to Limehouse, called at Yates as I passed.... came back to my Uncle's had tea there & came home wet through & very tired, having walked nearly 20 miles to-day.

12 AUG

My Uncle with Mr. Kennedy [*John Kennedy, the father of J.T. Pocock's late wife, Margaret, had owned and managed the famous Vineyard Nursery on the site of the modern Olympia at Hammersmith, which his father Lewis had founded, growing exotic, subtropical plants*] came down in the gig in the morning. Mr. K. wishes to take a house at Kilbourne, Mr. Jay sent my Mother three box tickets for the Cobourg Theatre [*later to be renamed the Old Vic*], she therefore went with Miss Underwood & myself & we were well entertained, saw three pieces *The Fatal Armour, Village Lawyer,* & *The Galley Slaves.* Returned highly delighted with the night's amusement.

14 AUG

At home doing my garden & Papa's walk all day.

15 AUG

My Father & I went to Chappell's Musical Repository in New Bond Street, we there met a musical belle to whom my Father had in his younger days been very attentive, she expressed her surprise at meeting him in a *music* shop & continued some smart raillery on the occurrence.

20 AUG

Went with my Father to Chappell's in the morning, then to Maddox Street & afterwards by appointment to Mr. Fowler, surgeon & apothecary, Seymour

Street, St. Pancras. Here we met Mr. Ryder & his partner for whom my Father made a good bargain, they took the lease of the house & drugs etc., at a valuation. I came home to dinner & my Father to tea very poorly. Miss Coney gave a singing party to some young ladies and gentlemen. My Father and I too – thought it very thoughtless and unkind their not inviting me.

21 AUG

Mr. Bilney has left Garrett's & commenced a school under the cognomen of 'Mentor Lodge' at Kensal Green, on the Harrow Road. He came in the aftn. to see his ducky, deary - o! & stayed to tea when they had two rubbers at whist. As he was afraid to go down the shady lane alone I went home with him & remained all night. If Jonah as Sambro says "was the devil of a fellow for *fish*" I think he has an equal in Bilney "who is a devil of a fellow for *flesh*". After eating a very hearty supper at hour house, on our arrival at his own he commenced a valorous attack upon a cold joint of beef & sundries, finishing the repast with a pound or two avordupois of cold pudding!

22 AUG

Came home early. A pianoforte came for the School from Chappell's.

23 AUG

To Ryder's with my Father. Wake, his partner, has "gone out" for want of money.

24 AUG, Sunday

It being a wet morning, none of us went to Church, but read prayers at home instead. I walked to Cochrane Terrace with Papa in the evening, when we returned across the fields, found Mr. and Mrs Shackle at our gate in their chaise, they invited my Father to dinner to-morrow.

25 AUG, Monday

With my Father in the morning to Carey Street, also went to my Uncle who invited me to dine with him on Wednesday saying *he* should do something for me.

27 AUG

To Mr. Bilney in the morning who taught me in cyphering [*arithmetic*] etc, left him at ½ past 1 oclk & went to my Uncle with whom I dined along with my cousins, after which he gave me a letter directed to my schoolmaster my Father liked, in which he promised to pay £15. for finishing my education until Christmas. My Father is going to Worthing to survey a house for Mr. Shackle.

28 AUG

My Father and Mr. Shackle left for Worthing early a.m. I went to school and did plenty of writing and cyphering.

29 AUG

Mr. Bilney wished me to get him a sharp dog, found one in the road & took it to him in the afternoon, if he is not naturally *sharp* he soon will be with Mr. B.

31 AUG, Sunday

After staying with Josiah Wright, left Bishopsgate early, went first to Bromley in Kent, 10 miles from his house, then across the fields to Beckenham, afterwards to the pretty little town of Sydenham, next Croydon, through shady Camberwell to Brixton where we had tea with the Underwoods & recounted our day's adventure. On coming back we found we had walked 25 miles *for pleasure*. What would your milksop cockney apprentices say to this?

[*I shall long remember the beautiful view which burst upon my sight, I think near Croydon, we had been traversing a dull bye road, when suddenly we came into the main road & crossed a bridge which was thrown over a beautiful winding canal. I stopped to gaze on the enchanting view, & could hardly be persuaded it was not a fairy scene, for I could hardly imagine so beautiful a place on earth; the clear winding sheet of water extended nearly as far as the eye could view, its banks were covered with weeping willows & rows of majestic elms were seen beyond them, while here & there from among the green trees were to be seen the lofty mansion of some great man, or the pretty white lodge of the retired citizen; a few swans that seemed to move by magic in the glass like water, not a little enlivened the scene, the canal was literally covered with boats, some sailing & some rowing, the sylph-like forms of the young & gay fair ones in their light summer dress reminded me of the fairy queens of olden times & I envied the 'gallant gay Lotharios' not a little who were conducting them.* John Pocock, 1835.]

3 SEP

Mr. Bilney as a favour asked me to buy fish hooks for him & boys at Paddington & treated me to some; on coming home along the Regent's Canal I threw my line in & directly pulled out a fin roach. My Father came home to-night having been at Worthing & Brighton also.

4 SEP

To Mr. Bilney's early when with Mr. Hall for our guide, Mr. Bilney & the whole school left home on an angling excursion, armed with *hooks & crooks*, sad implements of carnage amongst the finney tribe. Mr. H. took us along the Harrow Road to the River Brent, a very shallow stream, but we had a very little sport, and continued along the river until we came up to the Grand Junction Canal [*opened in 1801, later became part of the Grand Union Canal*], here the Brent runs *under* the canal, & I do not remember seeing anything so dark & terrible as the water just here. Like my Mother, who, it is prophesied, will be drowned, I also have an instinctive horror of water. We returned slowly along the canal having had a very bad day of it. Stayed tea.

5 SEP

Mr. Bennett came to breakfast in the morning & walked with my Father and self to Paddington. I met my Father again in the City. We went to Todd's, the large linen drapers etc. Here Papa bought me a neck handkerchief & gloves. He rode home very unwell.

6 SEP

Stayed to dinner with Mr. B. after which we went to the Canal & cast our lines in, it would be tedious to *enumerate* the *number* of fish we caught. "Hist, hist, bite!" says I, but the rascals wouldn't bite!

7 SEP

Went in the afternoon to the Gurneys who now live in the Abbey Road, stayed to tea. When Tom & Fred were returning across the fields with me, we met my Mother & Father & children with whom we returned to Gurneys. Went with Fred as far as St. John's Wood Chapel, when we all came home together – a lovely evening.

8 SEP

Tried the Bourne or Brook in the morning for eels but caught none, to the Canal in the afternoon with equal unsuccess.

9 SEP

To school as usual, am getting on famously in arithmetic.

10 SEP

To town with my Father in the morning & dined with him in the evening & I returned with him. My Father has decided I shall go to Bilney's as a boarder for six months on Saturday next, this is to finish my education and at the expiration of that time it is thought my Uncle will take me in his office. I am not to learn any more Latin to but to attend particularly to book-keeping. I am also to learn drawing and dancing.

15 SEP

Had to set to in right earnest in the morning. Although so near home, I am so childish that I feel the separation as bitterly as ever. I am ashamed to confess that I hate school with as much cordiality as I love *HOME*. I fear I shall never make a bright man & I am positive never a *learned* one, if my dear Mother & Father were less kind & less affectionate than they are it would perhaps prove a blessing to me hereafter. Went home in the afternoon to fetch my lines.

16 SEP

Walked in the fields with Mr. Bilney & boys after school hours, played at trap, bat & ball with them.

17 SEP

Sticking close to Arithmetic, just finishing the Double rule of three.

18 SEP

Our drawing master, Mr. Weeden, came at 9 o'clk, he says I make great progress & was much pleased with me. I think I shall be very fond of drawing & am determined to beat *sweet Miss* alias *Master Thomas* Hall who commenced with me; my sister Emily came in the morning with my clean linen. After school I went to my Uncle, St. Bride's Wharf, with a note from Mr. Bilney.

20 SEP, Saturday

Drawing day, got on capitally. My sister came in the morning & I went home after school hours, quite glad to see my Mother who went to town in the 2 o'clk stage with Maria, after tea William Robinson & self went to Josiah Wright who returned with us both slept at our house.

21 SEP

Walked with Josiah in the morning through Hampstead to Highgate, where we hired two donkeys to carry us home. The rascal of a boy neglected to tighten the girths of the one I rode, in consequence of which in going down hill, the saddle shifted first upon the neck & then upon the head of the beast, and of course I shifted with it until both went over his head together amid a roar of laughter from Josiah & some others who were on the road. Fortunately I was not hurt although the donkey ran over me. I mounted the brute again who took it into his head to gallop full tear, down a very steep hill, now I am not a good rider & never rode any horse but Papa's good 'Old Jack' so it cannot be wondered that I should not keep on. Old Nick himself could not stop the beast, & he took me up against a wall which he began rubbing my legs against unmercifully so I thought it best to fall off, by way of saving him the trouble of throwing me off. Josiah was convulsed with laughter & although my hand was torn a little & my new pair of black kid gloves quite spoiled, I could not forebear laughing also, though not quite so heartily as himself. I was determined however not to be done by a donkey, so I mounted him a third time & made the rogue carry me home in style. After tea Josiah & I walked up the village to fetch Eliza from Miss Coney's. Fred Gurney came in the evening & remained for supper. I walked with them to the New Road & Fred came back to St. John's Wood where we parted.

22 SEP, Monday
Fred Gurney walked up at 6 o'clk in the morning to see me. I returned to school immediately after breakfast.

23 SEP
Mr. Bilney went out at 12 o'clk leaving Mr. Monk to mind the school. He was very cross with me in the afternoon but I attribute this to his having visited The Plough of Harrow public house twice.

24 SEP
Took a rural walk over the fields with Mr. Bilney & the boys & Miss Coney, we came out on the Edgware Road when Miss C. left us & we returned.

25 SEP
Drawing in the morning, after School I went to Holborn to purchase me a pair of pumps and bluchers [*high-laced shoes named after Field Marshal Blücher*]. Also to Monk's wretched lodgings in James Town [*off Chalk Farm Road*] for Mr. Bilney.

27 SEP
Getting on with my drawings capitally. Mr. Bilney went out & Mr. Weeden remained in his place. I went home for my clean linen. Lewis & Maria are very ill with the whooping cough and my Father unwell, he was particularly low spirited and in writing down what I was to learn, he shocked me by adding "he did not think he should live until I left school." I came back with a heavy heart for I never heard Papa talk so despairingly before. I hope his fears are groundless; God only knows & may his 'Will be done'.

29 SEP, Sunday
A Holiday. Mr. Bilney, our worthy pedagogue, being united 'for better or worse' to Miss Charlotte Coney this day at Hampstead Church. I went to Paddington in the morning and then home. Walked to Tottenham Court Road with my Father.

1 OCT
Mr. B. sent for me in the morning, I went to Hampstead Heath with Mrs. Price, Emily and Eliza where we had much fun with the donkeys. Mrs. Price is a baby & no more fit to be the wife of a man of 70 than my little sister Maria; returned to School in the evening.

3 OCT

Had a good game at skittles in playhouse with Baker & others.

4 OCT

A wet day, Mr. B. out, made up my cuttings in scrap book.

5 OCT, Sunday

To Paddington church in the morning & for a walk to Kilburn in the afternoon, called at our house.

6 OCT

Mr. B. Promised us a treat, Miss Coney's School coming on Wednesday evening to dance with us.

8 OCT

Tom Hall, self & other boys, went to meet the young ladies whom we found on the road near Vere's. I tendered Miss Fowler my arm, & conducted her to our School, she is a pretty girl but unfortunately she knows this. She is the daughter of Mr. Fowler the surgeon, who is practising in Kilburn. We immediately recognised each other as she was present when my Father purchased the shop in Euston Square for Misses Rider of Wake; had some fun on our return and a few quadrilles, but the best of the fun was seeing the young ladies home again, a gentleman is particularly '*sweet*' with Miss Coney.

20. St Mary's church, Paddington, in 1805.

9 Oct

Went with Greathouse to Shepherds Bush to order some potatoes, crossed a winding brook 6 times & were much splashed etc.

11 Oct

Very poorly in the afternoon, had tea in the parlour with Mrs. Bilney.

13 Oct

Walked nearly to the top of the lane with Mr. B. & the boys.... Mrs. B., kindly gave us some cake & wine.

14 Oct

Drawing day, I have a beautiful study on hand.

15 Oct

Dancing day, took the head of the class. Mr. Upton tells me I shall make a good dancer.

16 Oct

Half Holiday & drawing day, very fond of Mr. Weeden.

17 Oct

The routine of lessons and scholdings, alternately, as usual.

20 Oct

Tom Hall's birthday. The pet lamb came in the afternoon with his Mother, sisters, *cake* etc. Drank his health in a good glass of port wishing many happy returns of the cake and wine.

24 Oct

Mr. and Mrs. B. Went out in the aftn. Mr. Weeden left in charge of us, attempted to sketch Merton Lodge [*the real name of 'Mentor Lodge', the Bilney's school; see entry for 21 August*].

28 Oct

A grand fuss with Smeathman who was convicted of breaking 4 panes of glass *for sport.*

29 Oct

A Regular Row with me, all the family rose up in arms, Mrs. Bilney Senior having declared I made "wry faces" etc., at her, Mr. & Mrs. B. just took me seriously to task; it is true she saw me making faces but not at her.

30 OCT

Mrs. Bilney Jnr. called me in the parlour & shaking hands requested me to think no more of yesterday's row, the old lady too shook my hand & gave me a kiss. P.S. I would rather by half Mrs. B. Jnr. had given the kiss than the old dame. Walked to Harlesdon Green in the afternoon.

1 NOV

Dancing day. Drew for amusement 'Sir Francis Burdett's Seat in Wiltshire'.

3 NOV

My sisters called in the morning, after dinner Mrs. Bilney, Catchpole, Baker, self & others went to Miss Coney's where we spent the night with the young ladies. My sisters were of the party, went home with them & rapped hard at the door then ran down the lane to School.

4 NOV

Dancing day. Mr. Upton says we shall be able to dance quadrilles well at Christmas. Troubled with a sore throat.

8 NOV

Dancing Day, getting on with our quadrille steps.

10 NOV

To Paddington in the morning with Papa, young Wells & self, started to see the Lord Mayor's Show, posted off to Golden Square for a friend of his, then to the Tower & Fenchurch Str. where we had an excellent view of the procession from my Father's range of Offices, then to St. Bride's Wharf, saw my Uncle. Samuel is confined with smallpox. Mr. Shackle & Mr Hall were on the barges & seemed to have entered into a *bad Speculation* owing to Samuel's illness. No one was admitted in the house and therefore there was *no dinner party* as usual. I waited one hour on Blackfriars Bridge before I could get over, so dense was the throng of people.

13 NOV

Walked to Kilburn with the School after hours, then to Maida Hill & along the Canal home.

15 NOV

.... My Father still very ill, he has some complaint which baffles the skill of all the doctors.

16 NOV

Tom Hall and self went to Paddington Church; Mr. B. thought it too wet for the little boys, who stayed at home. A miserable, dull afternoon; very glad when bed-time arrived.

17 NOV

Mr. Monk's Latin day, he gave me a long lesson in my much neglected *dead* language.

18 NOV

Drawing day. I have the prettiest piece to do seen as yet.

19 NOV

Miss Coney's young ladies came to practise dancing with us in the afternoon. Tom Hall and self walked back with them to Kilburn.

20 NOV

Tom Hall and self walked to Miss Coney's to fetch Mrs. Bilney, we escorted her home in style after dusk.

24 NOV

Home directly after breakfast for linen, did not stay five minutes, my poor Father is yet extremely ill and no one knows his complaint.

25 NOV

Went to Crawford Street with Hall after dinner to buy some gloves.

26 NOV

Had a dreadful pain in my side, no sleep last night.

27 NOV

Pain much worse, I could hardly get through the drawing lesson. Mr. B. sent the servant home with me. I went up to Dr. Rogers & he gave me some medicine to take every 6 hours.

29 NOV

Much better, pain less violent in the evening. Papa nursed me & I nursed him, both ill.

30 NOV, Sunday

To Church with my brothers & sisters in St. James St., Paddington, also some of the Kingcombe's children who behaved very ill. My pain came on in church and continued all aftn.

1 DEC

Sister Emily's birthday, went with her to Miss Coney's to dance. Upton was there & was furious with me for taking Miss Cousins down a country dance too fast for his fiddle to keep pace with us. Had *tea* there then came home & had some worthy of the name of tea.

4 DEC

Mr. Bilney, all the boys & the young ladies with Miss Coney went to the Zoological Gardens in the Regents Park [*opened in April, 1827*], returning we called at our house where my Mother divided a large basket of oranges amongst us.

7 DEC, Sunday

Sisters not at Church. We took a walk to Harlesdon Green in the afternoon. I am miserably dull here upon Sundays.

8 DEC

Hall & self walked to Kilburn to meet the young ladies. We had little dancing, played at cards *for love*.

9 DEC

Wrote my holiday letter home, which will do.

10 DEC

Wrote a school letter to my Uncle which is pronounced good enough to be forwarded to him.

11 DEC

With Wellstead & 2 Bakers to Harlesdon Green for a run with our hoops after school.

12 DEC

My birthday. I am now *14* years old, it is high time for me to be learning some trade or profession.

13 DEC

Poetically mad in the afternoon, commenced & finished a parody on 'When the rose of morn appearing' – Shocking!

14 DEC, Sunday

To church solus, Mr. B. deeming it too wet for the *boys* to go. My sisters fetched me home in the afternoon to see Mr. Udale who was a great friend to George at St. Helena. He is an excellent performer & delighted us with a recital of the pathetic piece of poetry *Eliza* & also poor *Betty*.

16 DEC
Mr. Bilney very cross all day, to Willesden with our hoops p.m.

17 DEC
Packing up books in a bustle, as we break up to-morrow.

18 DEC
Came home before any of the boys.

19 DEC
To Battle Bridge [*one of J.T. Pocock's estates for development was at Battle Bridge, an area now renamed King's Cross*] with my Father, met Lewis Pocock by Portland Road, left my Father in stage, then called at Haywards on my road to my Uncle, with whom I stayed [*to*] dinner & tea.

20 DEC
Mr. Bilney called in the morning. My Father having given me a lesson in Indian Ink drawing, I attempted a sketch which employed the greater part of the day.

21 DEC, Sunday
Left home in the morning according to appointment to see Josiah Wright, & met him (very poorly) with his Mother in Finsbury Square on the way to a chemist at Hoxton. I walked there with them & stayed with Josiah at home all day coming home after tea.

22 DEC
Drawing nearly the whole day, I am very pleased with Indian ink....

23 DEC
Left home at 11 oclk walked to Grays Inn... [*various places*].... & lastly to my Uncle who made me stay to tea, brought home some birdseed for Mama's goldfinch & a queer work entitled *Knickerbocker* which I am to read for Papa's amusement.

24 DEC
At home drawing all the morning. Miss Coney and Cousins and Mr. and Mrs. Shackles came in the evening when we played Pope Joan. Saw the young ladies home.

25 DEC
Christmas Day, had for dinner a very large piece of roast beef & a giant-like plum pudding.

21. Surviving in 1995: 18 Greville Place – formerly No. 6 – was built by George Pocock as a country house for his brother, John, of St Bride's Wharf.

26 DEC
My cousins Betsy & Lewis Pocock & Martha Bartlett came in the morning to see Radford's house which my Uncle has taken of him, intending to keep a country house. [*This was the semi-detached 6 Greville Place, which is believed to have been the present No. 18, much modernised and with a garage in the basement. A similar house was the cause of protests in the 1930s when a developer - the father of the present Lord Palumbo - demolished one half of the pedimented pair and replaced it with a block of flats.*]

27 DEC
Called upon Uncle & after tea rode from Fleet Street to Tyburn Gate on our way home.

29 DEC, Sunday
My Uncle came in the morning to take possession of his house.

31 DEC
Left home early, went to see Josiah who is very ill indeed, stayed some time with him; he is not however confined to his room.... dined with my Uncle, his birthday.

Chapter Five

Death of a Friend

1 JAN, 1829
In the evening, playing whist.

4 JAN, Sunday
Being a wet day we read prayers at home.

5 JAN
I went to Kingcombes & found Mrs. K. very lonely she put by her needle work & we also played at cards, I beat in every game.

7 JAN
To Captn. Murray before breakfast who I saw, copied an agreement between Walpole Eyre Esq., & my Father.

8 JAN
Took the agreement to Walpole Eyre's offices in the morning & brought home another to copy....

9 JAN
The usual *family broils* in full glory but this is quite stale.

10 JAN
To my Uncle's Office in the morning, saw Samuel who was very busy, went on to Price....

11 JAN, Sunday
To Paddington Church in the morning, the sexton took the clerk's place he read badly and called very 'wherry' – he also missed half the belief in repeating it which appeared 'wherry' bad.

20 JAN
Caught a handsome male chaffinch in my trap. Went to Paddington with George Kingcombe and purchased a cage.

22. Portobello farmhouse, Notting Hill. From a sepia drawing by W.E. Wellings.

21 JAN

Walked past Bello Porto farm [*Porto Bello House stood half a mile south-east of Kensal Green*] between Kensal Green and Bayswater on my road to Acton. Called upon Mr. Bilney with a letter from my father.

22 JAN

Mr. Underwood in the morning. He stayed to dinner after which he went with my father to see some land surveyed at Hampstead.

23 JAN

A couple of felts [*fieldfare*] as my father supposes them to be, in our garden all the morning. I fetched a gun from Twyford to have a crack at them but the wind being very strong they had left.

24 JAN

Caught a fine large black bird in my brick trap first thing in the morning. This is the male *felt* as pre-supposed. This fine bird together with a felt have from the severity of the Winter been starved out of the fields.

25 JAN, Sunday

With Emily, Tom and Lewis to Christ Church in the morning. Uncle called and saw my birds, and Miss Rogers, Samuel P., the Miss Bartletts and Robinson in an afternoon scramble.

26 JAN

Went to Homer Street, New Road with my father who kindly treated me with a cage for my blackbird.

28 JAN

To Miss Coney in the morning, who gave me a drawing lesson. Uncle fetched me in the evening to bring in a large basket full of tarts for us youngsters.

3 FEB

Started before breakfast in the morning to Islington to find a Mr. Hughes but in vain. I enquired to wit at 2 Public houses, four Chandlers shops, item two pot boys, 1 Cabinet maker, 2 butchers, 1 baker, 1 confectioner and 3 brats asliding, no Mr. Hughes.

4 FEB

....my Father endeavouring to sell his bricks at Kensington to Mr. Barnes of Paddington.

5 FEB

My Father decided & settled upon my returning to school as a day scholar on Monday next.

6 FEB

Called at Mr. Wright's to see Josiah who is still very ill.

7 FEB

To Paddington in the morning for my periodicals.

10 FEB

To School in the morning. Mr. Bilney having thrown the old schoolroom & little parlour into one makes a famous, large and commodious schoolroom.

11 FEB

To Mr. Bones in the morning, had a long hunt after Mr. Pearson concerning the bricks.

12 FEB

Half-Holiday. I am now in Fractions & am shortly going into book-keeping.

13 FEB

Went to school as usual. Had some fun with two black rascally old crows that usually perch on the tree close to the sharp angle of the lane. I frightened the scamps finely.

14 FEB

Saint Valentine's Day. I was amusing myself alone in the breakfast parlour in the evening when I heard the postman's double rap, directly after the servant came running upstairs with a letter for me saying it was a Valentine she knew. I immediately recognised in the direction the writing of Josiah Wright & under this impression wondered he had not disguised his writing, my fright & dismay was very great when instead of a Valentine I read the following letter, not from Josiah, but from his Father whose writing is the very counterpart of his own:

'Master John Pocock, Sir,
It is with great grief I have to inform you that my dear son Ralph & your companion departed this life last night at ½ past 9 oclk - without a groan and without a sigh - if you should have a wish to see him come down the first opportunity.
My best respects to you & Father & Mother & I hope you are all well.
Yours very truly,

13 Feb. 1829, Liverpool St.　　　　　　　*Wm. Wright.*

I was perfectly stupefied with horror & surprise, no occurrence could have taken place so unexpected, so unlooked for, I went downstairs with a heavy heart & gave the letter to my Mother for I could not tell her the intelligence myself, on reading the letter she exclaimed, "Oh, John" almost in a reproachful tone, and those two words cut me to the quick, for my conscience told me I had neglected him though unwittingly. As my Father was in a precarious state of health at the time my Mother carefully & gently acquainted him with the news, while I went to Paddington with my sisters; he was equally astonished as ourselves & was indignant with them all in not acquainting me with his approaching dissolution. [*In bidding a long & last adieu to my kind and generous friend Josiah Ralph Wright I cannot do so without a self accusing spirit of regret, which regret I shall experience as long as memory exists; I am sorry, very sorry, I was not with him in his last moments but little indeed did I suppose his illness of so dangerous a nature; the exceedingly cold and uncivil reception I met with from the other inmates of the house when I called & the denial of his Father's clerk, when I wished to see him, only a few days before he died, burst my pride & I felt piqued at being refused to visit him for whom I had the warmest affection & esteem, & who I am sure liked me equally well: this regret is heightened by the circumstance communicated to me by Ward, his nurse, namely, that the very day I called he, Josiah, was repeating my name from morn to night, both in his paroxysisms of delirium & when in his senses, he very much wished to see me before he died, & I am but too well assured that Josiah left this world under the conviction that I, his principal, his sole friend had deserted him in his last moments. Such a feeling, (so far from real) I would not have had him suppose for all the world. Josiah is in a happier sphere, and now that he has put on immortality, may be reading my heart & see there that my friendship for him was as fresh & strong when he died as it was when he was in perfect health. Peace be to his ashes! &*

may I be called to another & a better world with as clear and unsullied a conscience as that which he left this with. John Pocock 1835.]

15 FEB, Sunday
Walked to Holloway with my Uncle in the morning, went to several persons there with him & heard a long dissertation upon flues & chimneys, we then took some luncheon at an Inn when I left him & proceeded to Liverpool Street, but found the house shut up & empty save the corpse of my poor friend whose ever ready hand when alone to open the door to me could not perform that office now; I then went to Coleman Street for my Father's medicine.

16 FEB
Went to Mr. Wright in the morning & saw the remains of poor Josiah, Oh that such a fine manly form should be snapped off in the flower of youth, he had just attained his twentieth year & was as fine and healthy a young man as would be seen in a day's journey. He was about six feet high & his robust frame well apportioned in every respect, I took hold of his pale clammy hand & musing on the finger that had written many a kind & generous letter to me though those fingers would never dictate the feelings of his open sympathising heart more.

17 FEB
Went to school as usual. Mr. Bilney wishes to take me as teacher but my Father will not submit me to the drudgery of an academy.

18 FEB
To school, I am to go into Book-keeping this week.

19 FEB
After school I walked to Mr. Wright's to ask concerning when the funeral is to take place & was told that I should receive a letter about it, afterwards I went to Long Acre to buy some copy books for Mr. Bilney.

20 FEB
A beautiful stag, hunted by His Majesty's hounds & about 60 riders of distinction passed our schoolroom windows. He made off for Kilburn & was turned close by our house. The whole neighbourhood presented a very lively appearance from the number of hunstmen in their scarlet coats, the stag set off in the direction of Paddington & coming to the Grand Junction Canal swam across towards the church, it so happened the door was open and he bounded in and was caught *inside the church*! The poor creature who was a victim to this inhuman sport must have given chase at least 35 miles as he was started at Hounslow & had made a long circuitous route.

23. St Botolph's, Bishopsgate, where Josiah Wright was buried in the churchyard.

Received a funeral letter from poor Josiah's undertaker for tomorrow, which I will certainly attend as being the last tribute of affection I can pay my last best friend.

21 FEB, Saturday.
Left home with my Father & Mr. Marling in the chaise which I left at Tyburn & walked through the City to Mr. Wright's.... the funeral left at ½ past 3 for Bishopsgate Churchyard distant 3 minutes walk only. Poor Josiah is buried close to the side of the Church & very near the active thoroughfare of noisy Bishopsgate Street. I could have wished a more sequestered spot; Mr. W. & Ward very much affected, Josiah had been a kind master to Ward [*servant*] when he broke his leg and visited him every day in the hospital besides supplying him with cash to purchase niceties, etc. Surely one possessed of so good a soul & so good a heart will readily find admission into Heaven! Honest & upright as man could be, generous & free as sympathising in the sufferings of others, and as prompt & ready to help the unfortunate as he.

22 FEB, Sunday
Mr. Wright called in the afternoon, it appears Josiah died of Typhus fever.

23 FEB
Went early in the morning with my Father to Sir John Lillies, Northend, then to Mr. Carters, Walham Green, then back to Sir John. Saw Mr. Pagett & rode home in the chaise with Mr. Morley.

24 FEB

My Mother very unwell [*Hannah Pocock's last child was born two months later*], Phoebe Underwood came in the afternoon, when she was seized with an hysterical fit.

28 FEB

To Paddington with Kingcombe, got the last numbers of Allen's *History of London*.

1 MAR, Sunday

Our new Chapel opened this day [*probably the chapel in the centre of Kilburn Square, since demolished*], the little village of Kilburn never looked so lively or so proud as on this day, we had an excellent sermon adapted to the occasion by the Rev. Mr. Hancock who is appointed Minister, this Chapel is intended as a Chapel of Ease to Hampstead but owing to some irregularity the bishop of London refuses to consecrate it, in consequence of which it became necessary to make some slight alteration from the established form of prayer of the Church of England which was observed; we have long wanted a place of worship as the nearest church is distant 2 miles, the Chapel itself is an elegant, large & commodious structure, the organ a very fine one, the pews well arranged etc., altogether it will be a great blessing to the place & is likely to enhance the value of all the property in the neighbourhood.

10 MAR, Sunday

Early to Camden Town for Holbrook the Surveyor on my Father's site who came soon after & met Walpole Eyre and Mr. Shaw Junr. his surveyor on the field my Father is about purchasing, which they measured. Holbrook is a very clever young man, he served his time to Dent. My Father had dinner prepared for him at the Red Lion where we accompanied him. Mr Father wishes to run Greville Place Road into the Abbey Road through this field & has consulted with Messrs. Hall & Ward the large landed proprietors who approve of the plan.

11 MAR

To school. In the afternoon I tied some feathers on pack thread & hung it across the beds in my Uncle's garden to prevent the birds picking out the seeds.

12 MAR

To school in the morning. My cousin Samuel goes to France with Mr. Kennedy to-morrow, for the benefit of his health.

13 MAR

Mr and Mrs Shackle to tea and afterwards played a rubber. While so doing my Uncle came in from town & informed us that while talking at the Coal Mart with

Mr. Smith a retail Merchant & one of his heaviest creditors, he suddenly dropped down & expired, seized with a paralytic stroke, my Uncle is a loser of £3000 by it.

15 MAR, Sunday
Mrs. Milder took Emily home on a week's visit. Eliza is seriously ill with the measles.

16 MAR
To school. My Father desires I may learn Book-keeping only, as he intends I should leave on Lady Day.

18 MAR
Resumed my game of fright in our own garden today.

17 MAR
Finished my Uncle's garden with regard to the feather system [*bird-scaring*], he called in the evening. Eliza is a little better.

19 MAR
Mr. Bilney asked me to come in the evening, I would not & did not go.

20 MAR
Mr. Bilney rather cross at my non appearance yesternight, he said he "knew why I would not come, because I had forgotten my Dance steps & was ashamed to dance before Mr. Upton"! Pshaw, the fact is I do not like his sham parties. Eliza is much better.

24 MAR
Mr. B. is getting fat, I wish the increase of good temper would keep pace with increase of body.

28 MAR
Went to town with my Father early. Mrs. and Mr. Rogers took a 'friendly cup of *tay*' with us.

29 MAR, Sunday
Walked to Carters, Walham Green in the afternoon, took tea with Miss C. who was arrayed in all her finery for Church....

30 MARCH to 4 APR
Myself very unwell, headache, shivering etc. Father very poorly with bad cough. Dr. Rogers sent him some medicine.

Chapter Six

Helping Father

5 APR, 1829

My Father's disorder increased most alarmingly.

6 APR

Uncle called, my Father very, very bad & none of the physicians can tell what his complaint is, or relieve him.

7 APR

Phoebe Underwood is very kind to my Mother, who needs much her friendship.

9 APR

To the City for my Father, took an advertisement concerning our bricks to the *Morning Advertiser* Office, Strand & then went to the wharf & to Bouverie St.

10 APR

Mrs. Wright [*Josiah's mother*] called. I went on the road to Paddington with her, she told me Josiah had become very religious towards his end which much gratified me in hearing. Went to school to-day for the last time, finished Journal in Double Entry.

[*I cannot register my last school day without glad feelings of shame & regret, shame that I did not employ my time to more advantage; & regret that my parents' extreme affection for me should have distracted my attention almost entirely from scholastic pursuits. I was always considered a dull boy (a bye term for a fool), 'Glump' & 'Old Steady' were my nicknames, & these names I more than merited. I never liked school, far from it, I detested the very word, & the gigantic green letters on Mr. Garrett's House, KINGSTON HOUSE ACADEMY always made me in a panic. I ever went to School with a clouded face & returned home with a pleasant one, when a boarder at Garrett's (which I was several years) I generally contrived to get home on the Saturday afternoon under the plausible pretence of staying Sunday at home with my sisters & on these occasions it rarely occurred that Kingston House Academy discovered me its inmate before the Monday night or Tuesday following when my mind lingering on past pleasures was totally unfit for study and yet I never got punished for these delinquencies for I remember having one sound caning only & I never had the honour or 'Mounting the horse' as birching was generally designated. I cannot tell how it occurred but I was a general favourite with Mr. Garrett & the teachers for I gave them no trouble or anxiety.*

Mr. G. was always holding me forward as an example to the other brats & Mrs. G. would often let out a passing euconium on 'Old Steady' as she termed me, then I managed to get 2 or 3 birthdays per annum & could fix a birthday for one of my brothers or sisters whenever I pleased, & my Mother was too fond of me to complain of this chicanery; then again, I was rather a sickly boy and could be 'very ill' pro re rata aye, & remain so too, this all passed off very well.

I was once kept away from School six months, & on my return as a day scholar my Father wanted me so constantly in the City, that my attendance at School did not average 4 days per week, & the little I learned in those four days was as readily forgotten in the other three. The Latin tongue I denounced as a 'crackjaw dead language' and as I would not be a rogue of a doctor! or lawyer I cared little or nothing about it, the only part of my education that might be said to keep time with my years was arithmetic & this branch was totally useless to me in the medical profession. Nothing would do for me but 'Home, Sweet Home! There's no place like home', says I & much cause have I to repent this foolish partiality.

A boy who is intended to become anything of a scholar, must be sent away entirely from his parents, their kindness is a bane which will wreck his mind, their affection is destruction and an insurmountable barrier to his progress in life, & so it proved with me, thus at the age of 14 years & 4 months I was taken from school a mere idiot, I could not write passably, I could not dictate a letter or spell with any accuracy. I was like a young plant that had been taken from the bed & transplanted too soon, my Father's illness & his unsettled varying ideas as to what profession or trade I was to follow were great drawbacks to me, & although years have convinced me of my sad deficiency in knowledge, and although I have made many efforts to repair my slender learning, still I feel my ill-conducted education will be an impediment to me as long as I live. John Pocock, 1835]

13 APR

In the morning to Mrs. Brown [*Josiah's sister*] who was to have gone with me to Westley's to procure me Josiah's situation, she referred me to her Mother who also felt too much affected to go. Mr. W. promised if I came to-morrow.

14 APR

To Liverpool Street. Mr. Wright and myself went to Westley's who was from home. Walked home very fatigued.

17 APR

Mr. Hewitt called in the morning, I rode with him to the Borough, called on Mr. Price who wishes me to superintend his timberyard. Mr Father is a little better.

18 APR

Walked with Tom & Lew to Sir Coutts Trotter, Willesden [*Brondesbury House near Kilburn was the country seat of Sir Coutts Trotter of Grosvenor Square*] in the morning for a turf acct. met Papa near Peter's who treated us with some raisins at Forest the Grocer.

19 APR, Sunday

To Chapel, had Bilney's large pew in the gallery entirely to myself, walked beyond Cricklewood with G. Kingcombe in the afternoon. My Father very ill again.

21 APR

Our family increased very early this morning when a new sister was brought into the world. [*This was Betsy, who was not to be baptised until 1837*]. I & Uncle went home with Dr. Rogers at daybreak.

22 APR

A wet day. To Maida Hill in the morning. Mama is doing 'as well as can be expected' to use the nurse's own words.

23 APR

My Father went in the gig accompanied by my Uncle to young Dr. Latham who pronounces his complaint to be 'an affection of the heart' this is a vague definition, he advises cupping [*a technique for bleeding, or pain-relief*].

24 APR

To Paddington to arrange with a cupper.

25 APR

Mr. Heath came in the morning & cupped my Father between the shoulders, Mr. H. observed it would do him good. "Yes", replied Papa (while his pale cheeks assumed a paper hue while he spoke) "it will do me good one way or another, for if I do not get better soon, I shall go into the other Country." It grieved me very· much to see my Father so mournful but I yet cling to the hope of his fears being without foundation.

27 APR

My Father a little better to-day.

1 MAY

Went to North End [*in Fulham*] to see the bricks put into the barge my Father having sold all but the bats to Mr. Buck. Smith the bargeman rowed me up the basin stream into the Thames and I landed at Vauxhall Bridge.

2 MAY

Hired Humphrey's fly in the morning when my Father & self set off first to Dr. Latham's residence, who was not at home, then to the Marshalls where we took lunch & next over Battersea Bridge to Mr. Price. Called for Groceries at Paddington.

24. *'London going out of Town....or, The March of Bricks and Mortar!' George Cruikshank's vision of the relentless expansion of London by such developers as the Pococks in 1829. The signpost points to Hampstead, so Kilburn Priory villas must be the new buildings in the distance.*

3 May

Went to Chapel in the morning, I like Mr. Hancock's preaching, his sermon today was particularly impressive and delivered in a fluent, easy and able manner.

4 May

To North End in the morning, but the barge had not come up. My Father agreed with Mr. Price that I should go on Monday.

5 May

To North End again, the barge could not get into the Wharf, it is very bad to navigate.

6 May

To North End to see the bricks delivered, the barge came up and will be ready laden by to-morrow's tide.

7 May

Bricks laden, but no Mr. Buck to pay for them as by appointment so I detained them.

8 May

To North End in the morning, found the barge & cargo had sunk last night when the tide came up, so much for Mr. Buck. I still refused to let her go. Smith swore like a trooper, but it would not do.

9 MAY
Went to Dulwich with my Father & Mrs Kingcombe in Morley's fly, to get a settlement with Buck, whom we saw. Dulwich is a pretty little village.

10 MAY, Sunday
In the afternoon I went to Primrose Hill & Chalk Farm where I met Mr. K. & the children, & then went on with George Kingcombe to Oxford St. for my Father's medicine, on coming home I had the misfortune to lose the prescription for which act of carelessness I was deservingly upbraided but here it did not end. Mrs. Kingcombe (who loves to appear more shrewd & discerning than other people, or than she is herself) called George aside & asked how much I had paid for the Mixture, he replied eighteen pence, when I had in fact given 3/6. Of this she immediately informed my Father & Mother, when Mrs. Underwood was dispatched to know the fact, all this was unknown to me, my Father said in her absence, he would stake his existence that I had paid the full amount. Which on Phoebe's return proved to be the case, my Mother & Phoebe took my part very warmly; I do not thank Mrs. Kingcombe for her gross suspicions, or George for not looking sharper.

11 MAY
Went to Price's but did not stay as my father cannot spare me for a day or two.

13 MAY
Mr. Kingcombe, my Father, Eliza & self rode in Morley's double chaise first to Paddington, then to Eyres, Lucas & lastly Price, my destination where I arrived 3 p.m. with all my goods, chattles, wares, apparel etc. etc.

14 MAY
Engaged greater part of the day in the new house, taken by Mr. P. corner of Belvedere Road.

15 MAY
Mr. Kingcombe called in on me, my Father intends sending a lot of deals to our Yard, in which he may share the profits, at present there is nothing but mahogany.

16 MAY
Went to Apothecaries' Hall in the afternoon, & home in the evening. Saw my Uncle who says he will call some day at the Yard.

17 MAY, Sunday

To Chapel in the morning. Tom Gurney to dinner. Mrs. Kingcombe's infant was buried this afternoon. Tom walked with me as far as Westminster on my way back to Price.

18 MAY

Arranging the timber in yard all the day.

19 MAY

To Huberts, Lambeth, & Parliament Street for Mr. P. in the morning. Mr. Price is a *rum* one, he has been many years abroad, & spent some considerable time at Sierra Leone where all the people were dying about him like "sticks a breaking!" but he being a little piece of uncommon "stubborn stuff" weathered the storm & is a buxom, sprightly old beau of 70, his wife's age multiplied by 3¼ just makes his own. He brought a large cargo of mahogany home on his last trip, much of which, with subsequent additions is in the Yard still. He wishes to enlarge his business with the aid of my Father, to which business it is intended I may succeed but I think the old Gent is rather too fond of *rum* to be an able master for me.

21 MAY

Was to have gone to the Commercial Dock with Mr. P. to see some timber, but did not. Went home in the afternoon. Miss Rogers (two) called & offered us some tickets for the theatre, but we preferred staying at home. Mr. Murrell, Mr. & Mrs. Kingcombe joined us in the evening, in a pleasant game at Loo.

22 MAY

Left home with my Father in Morley's chaise, left him in Dean Street, Soho, & took a letter from him to Mr. Cocker, no change has taken place in the office. I met my Father again in Bride Lane, when we rode to Price, & went with him to the Grand Surrey Canal Dock, Rotherhithe, to see some timber which will be sold to-night. Mr Price & my Father then rode to the London Tavern, City, where I met them & the sale took place (by the candle) [*the bidding was stopped when a candle had burned down to a pre-set pin*] at ½ past 6 o'clk every lot of wood we wanted fetched enormous prices, which is unaccountable in the present depressed state of the timber trade. We left my Father at the Bank & then returned.

25 MAY

Went with my Father & brothers to see Cousin Betsy who filled our pockets with cakes, I then set off to town & delivered a letter from my father in Grosvenor Square for the Right Honorable Mrs. Howard (lady of Colonel) [*wife of the Hon. Fulke Greville Howard, a business associate of George Pocock's, who was brother of Viscount Templeton and who lived at 7 Grosvenor Place and at Levens Park, Westmorland*], then to Gray's Inn & to the yard. Phoebe Underwood had called wishing to see me, I therefore walked to Brixton & found the family in much distress about Mr. U. who had gone to Portsmouth, & promised to return on Friday.

26 MAY
In the large house, greater part of the day, men busy stencilling the walls, etc.

27 MAY
Mr. P. opened the old yard with the new one of the large house which makes a capacious place of it.

29 MAY
Oak Apple day, went to Westminster with Harry the boy.

30 MAY, Saturday
Went home in the evening, walked with Papa (who is improving in health to my delight) saw Uncle with whom we had a long chit chat.

3 JUN
Piling a large heap of blackwood greater part of the day.

4 JUN
Price has not half enough business for me. I like a very active business, & never to be at a stand still for occupying my time.

6 JUN, Saturday
Went home, found my Father very ill, this northerly wind does not agree with him.

8 JUN
Whit Monday. Out of 8 or 10 men employed by Mr. P. one only came 2 hours after time- and so-so. I've sent him 'back again'.

10 JUN
Mr. P. offered to let me go home in the aft. but I did not go.

11 JUN
Sawyers dug a pit & commenced on a large log of mahogany (beautiful vein).

13 JUN, Saturday
Went home before dinner, saw a letter from George which they received on Thursday. He writes very coolly & does not even mention his Mother, I shall schold him well for this.

14 JUN, Sunday

After dinner we were all sitting in the Long Parlour, with exception of Emily, who came breathless upstairs exclaiming, "Here's James Magson"! Who? We severally cried out each jumping up with the exclamation but he soon appeared to answer for himself, it appears his rupture became so bad at St. Helena that he was unfit for the Service, & was consequently invalided home, he arrived at Gravesend yesterday in *Earl of Balcarres* & came up the river in one of Company's yachts. he brought a china rice box for Mama & some shells, etc.

19 JUN

Mr. Price met my Uncle who came in to see our place, my Father called just at the time. My Uncle will see my Papa about me this evening.

20 JUN, Saturday

Home early in aftn. called on Uncle with my Father, he is very anxious to set me up in life, but does not like me to remain with Price, who would never teach me the achme of business. I shall therefore leave him soon. Fetched Betsy a volume of my Plays.

21 JUN, Sunday

Mrs. Kingcombe left Tower stairs in a Steamer Packet this morning for Dublin with her daughter Eliza to whom I gave a Bible and Gospel History. Little Eliza will remain in Ireland with a friend. Miss Edmonds took tea with us, she is a very accomplished lady & enlivened the evening with her conversation.

23 JUN

Rode the horse to Christie's near the Coburg Theatre in the afternoon.

27 JUN

This is the last day of my staying with Price.

28 JUN, Sunday

To Chapel in the morning with the young Kingcombes who behaved very rude. James Magson came to dinner, I walked to St. John's Wood with him on his return to town.

Chapter Seven

A Walk to Hastings

2 JUL, 1829
James Magson dined with us, I went to Lisson Grove with him returning an exceedingly wet day. Tom & Lew were breeched [*into long trousers*] to-day, they look a funny pair of little chaps, and are exceedingly proud of their pockets.

4 JUL
James Magson came in the morning & we cut some of the lower branches of the Poplar trees to stick the scarlet runners but did this very badly.

5 JUL, Sunday
To Chapel. After dinner I took a solitary but delightful walk to Edgware, & went down the lane as far as Whitchurch [*the seat of the Duke of Chandos*] this is a handsome Gothic structure, returned home, about sunset much pleased with my lonely ramble.

6 JUL
With James Magson to Bilney's, he is trying to get a teachers situation with him, we afterwards went to Paddington & met my Father & Mr. Jay who took Stage to Islington.

7 JUL
Dull wet day, remained at home from morn 'til night.

8 JUL
Magson called in the morning, having seen Mr. Bilney, I went with him to Fenchurch Street where we met my Father, with him to the Hope Coffee House, Fore Street. Left my Father at Fleet Market going to Underwoods as he leaves town soon for Hastings, sea air being recommended by his physicians.

10 JUL
Attended a trial at Westminster Hall, Pocock (J.T.) v. Russen, my Uncle lost not only this, but a second suit decided to-day, my Father was witness for defendant, we afterwards dined at an Hotel close by with Russen & witnesses, left my Father at Charing Cross on the Brixton stage.

11 JUL

Rode with my Uncle in his gig to Camden Town & Holloway, then to the Wharf, went to Noyes' & Gurneys', came back to the Wharf & rode home with him, stayed dinner with Betsy & him.

12 JUL, Sunday

After dinner walked to Brixton with my Mother. We saw my Father (who will leave for Hastings to-morrow) & all the Underwoods, rode back as far as Oxford Street.

13 JUL

To Paddington with Magson in the morning, he is engaged as teacher at Bilney's.

16 JUL

Rode with my Uncle to town, he wished much for me to go into his office but Samuel who is now a partner will not consent, he is kindly teaching me to drive, returned & dined with Betsy & him in the evening.

21 JUL

My brothers Tom & Lew & Edw. Kingcombe went with James to Bilney's in the morning. Moschelle the Italian composer left us to-day & will be succeeded by Mari the musician of Bond Street to-morrow. My Uncle & Betsy left London in the morning on an excursion to Southampton they will call on my Father at Hastings on their return.

22 JUL

Rode with Lewis Pocock in the chaise first to Notting Hill, then by the Thames to Hammersmith afterwards to Battcock at Chelsea got down at Hyde Park Corner & walked home. Went with my Mother to Crawford Street to buy a new carpet for the breakfast parlour. Mr. Price brought his pony to place with Morley at grass, the little man (always scheming) is much taken up with a machine for cutting wood to make band [*hat*] boxes.

23 JUL

With my Cousin Lewis in the morning, first to town then severally to Islington, Holloway, Highgate, Finchley & lastly to Whetstone where Lew had to inquire for the Revd. Mr. Harris, but being full of the place he very gravely asked a nursery maid for the Revd. Mr. Whetstone, the girl blushed & seemed confused, when he very innocently repeated the question, I could not keep my countenance any longer but burst out laughing in which he joined on detection of the error, when the girl turned sulkily away without deigning an answer as she must have thought we were making fun with her. On our return to the City I called at the offices, Fenchurch Street [*George Pocock's office had been in Fenchurch Street; presumably he had let it*] for the rent.

26 JUL, Sunday
Mr. Kingcombe & wife in the evening, he returned from Hastings last night & intends joining the proprietor of a newspaper just commencing there.

27 JUL
Went to Captain Murray in the morning & called upon Mr. Moschelle while in town. My Uncle returned from Hastings. My Father is very ill & lonely. I formed the idea of walking down to Hastings to see & assist him. My Uncle & Mother were pleased at my offer but seemed to have some misgivings upon my completing the long walk in 2 days.

28 JUL
At home all day, went to Uncle's in the evening, Mrs. Bartlett & daughter there [6 *Greville Place*]. He kindly gave me a sovereign to help me on the road & I slept with him so as to be awake & off early in the morning.

29 JUL
Up at 5 o'clk, rang Maria's bell who was awake & kindly waiting for me, bid her farewell, & proceeded on my journey. It commenced raining at Chapel Street, Paddington, & continued until I reached Lewisham, had breakfast at a coffee house in Greenwich Road. Cut J.P. on the old tree which supports one side of the stile in crossing the field just past Lewisham, here I had been before with my late friend Josiah Wright.

At Bromley I took some porter & here I began to feel the warmth of the weather, I had the company of a fellow traveller soon after which he made the time pass agreeably, I was much delighted with the beautiful view from a remarkably long & steep hill which I think my companion called Madame's Court Hill, here the eye is agreeably entertained with the most refreshing vernal scenes as far as the horizon, to the right hand a few miles distant in a beautiful sequestered vale, I perceived the noble Country Mansion of some great squire, or lord perhaps, the noble building of a dazzling white hue, with pointed spires, derived in pleasing contrast from the dark umbrage of the thickly set surrounding green trees. I long looked on the surrounding scene & quitted the place with regret.

Soon afterwards I lost my fellow traveller who struck off from the main road, I then passed through the little village of Riverhead & soon arrived in the populous town of Seven Oaks so named from the circumstance of seven fine oaks which (with exception of one which has withered away) are yet standing, here is a free school erected by Sir William Sevenoaks Lord Mayor of London in 1418 who is said to have been a foundling, charitably educated by a person of this town.

I rested at the Wheatsheaf & was obliged to partake of some bread & cheese (the latter *bad Dutch*) as they had no meat in the house and I could not wait their cooking any. I however regaled myself with some fine Kentish black-hearted cherries, on leaving the town the driver of a Hastings van rode me two miles on towards Tunbridge, which is 7 miles from Sevenoaks. There are several pretty seats on the road in the vicinity of Tunbridge which I failed not to remark, I passed through this old town with admiration, simply because it was ancient and I am such an old-fashioned fellow myself that I love anything that tells of the good 'olden times'.

Day was fast closing when I left this town and struck off on the dull high road to Hastings. I walked to an Inn two miles from the town where I intended to remain for the night, but was much disappointed that I could get no bed here & it was 4 miles on the road to the next public house, I thought it cowardly to turn back, and although very tired, in a strange country place, & night closing in I continued on the road, fear gave additional impulse to my footsteps & I continued at a rate I could not otherwise have maintained but for this feeling, as I had a large quantity of money for my Father as well as my own, I was in constant dread of being attacked and 'fancie' conjured bushes & brambles into highwaymen, however I determined to make a desperate resistance if attacked although entirely unarmed.

Thus I continued this long 4 miles (which appeared 6 to me) occasionally running, & then feeling if the money was safe which my Mother had carefully sewn in my pocket. With great joy after passing this deserted part of the country I perceived a light at the top of a hill before me & on coming up found it proceeded from Woodsgate Toll House. I speedily sought an inn close by, which however bore no resemblance to a public house but rather like a farmers place without sign or signature. I immediately went to bed for I had lost all appetite & was shown into a room with about fourteen beds in it, fortunately there was but one fellow traveller, for I hate sleeping with strangers. On calculating how far I had walked this day while lying in bed I found it exceeded *forty miles* & this shows what perseverance will do! My right foot gave me so much pain I could not sleep however for an hour after I retired.

30 JUL

Arose at ¼ to 6 a.m. & immediately continued my route to Hastings distant about 30 miles. I walked very lame at first, my right foot being very painful, had breakfast at Lamberhurst a small town or village on the road, after leaving, the road assumes a wild & desolate appearance, the dexter side is limited by a thick & ancient forest, the earth in many parts had separated in broad fissures leaving the naked roots & bare trunks of the old trees open to view; it rained heavily when I reached the second milestone from Lamberhurst, and, as there was no house adjacent I turned into the forest & sought shelter under a massey old oak whose lower branches were contorted nearly in a horizontal position, affording me a comfortable seat which the thick clear green moss rendered more inviting, here I remained above an hour, mid a multitude of thought; here away from the servile haunts of degraded man I had full leisure to soliliquise the beauties of nature, in her wildest, and to the most beautiful dress, here I had time to follow awhile the natural bent of my imagination & laud dame Nature & the lovely garb she wears, here as some poet had said,

> 'May Meditation think down hours to moments
> & learning wider grow without its books.'

I cut a large XXX on the old tree that sheltered me from the rain & continued along the dull monotonous road until my arrival at Robertsbridge, this town had 6 or 7 bridges thrown over as many small streams, I stopped at the George Inn & took some beer but could eat nothing, & then went on to the town of Battle. The Abbey (its name was enough) immediately attracted my attention and enquiries, this noble structure (which I had not time to examine) was erected by William the Conqueror A.D. 1066 in commemoration of his defeat over Harold, the field once the scene of unhallowed carnage, is now fairly spread with the green carpet of nature, and fine trees flourish with the soil once red with blood of hardiest Britons, the church I also saw and admired. Here I saw a van going to Hastings & I gladly paid the driver 1s. 6d. for the ride, we got into the town at sunset, raining hard at the time, we passed under a canopy or arch of green trees just on entering the town & then slushing through High Street stopped at the White Horse. I dismounted & speedily found Mrs. Wright's residence, No. 5 Caroline Place [*an elegant new terrace, named after Queen Caroline - estranged wife of George IV – who was popular in Hastings; below the castle, facing the beach and then said to be 'well defended from the Northern Blast and commands an excellent view of the Sea'; since demolished*], my Father was out when I arrived but came in while refreshing myself with a tea, he was much surprised & very pleased to see me. Retired early with him in much need of rest, but first wrote & posted a letter for my Mother acquainting her with my safe arrival, my father is still very bad.

31 JUL

Sauntered out on the beach after breakfast & soon perceived the ruins of the Castle which seemed almost perpendicular above me. I immediately visited the interior whose ancient ruins, though scanty, much pleased me, I also saw the grotto on the table of which among innumerable lot of initials & names I succeeded in deciphering that of my lost poor friend 'JOSª R. WRIGHT'. I put a very deeply cut 'P.1829' close to his name in the only vacant place I could find, the view of the sea & town with the surrounding country is very fine on account of his elevation from the ocean.

25. *Hastings, as John Pocock would have first seen it on the road from London, and All Saints' Church, which he sketched.*

1 AUG, Saturday

Went to the new town of 'St Leonard's' with my Father, this town consists of ranges of magnificent houses, laid out with much taste & style exhibiting some noble specimens of architecture mostly in the style of our new terraces in the Regent's Park, none of the houses were as yet complete but were in a state of great forwardness, the principal speculator on the elegant town is Mr. Burton the wealthy builder of Burton Crescent etc. [*St. Leonard's had been planned and designed as a fashionable seaside resort a mile to the west of Hastings by James Burton, father of Decimus, and building had begun in 1828; John Kennedy lived in Burton Crescent – now Cartwright Gardens, Bloomsbury.*] My Father knows him intimately having been a brother speculator in the wide world of bricks & mortar, the town is built on the site of William the Conqueror's landing place & near the Martello Towers.

At the invite of Mr. Peake, a fellow lodger, we returned to Caroline Place in his boat alongside the beach as Mrs. Wright's house faces the sea, we previously inspected a nicely constructed model of the Town, which was obligingly shown to us by the architect. Walked alone on the East Hill in the evening & returned along the Parade, when to my joy and surprise I met Henderson an old school fellow at Garretts coming up the flight of steps by the music stand, it appears he came down to Hastings for the purpose of seeing his mother & sister who have returned home leaving him for a week or so here.

2 AUG, Sunday
Bathed in the sea with Henderson at 7 a.m. near the White Rock. We removed our lodgings to Mr. Bellman's, Hastings Priory [*inland and uphill from Caroline Place*], as my Father was so uncomfortable at Wright's.

3 AUG
Walked with Henderson to Hollington church, distant four miles from town, it is an ancient small building, singularly situate in the centre of a wood, and no house within ¼ mile of it, the country parts about here are not nearly so lovely as about Kilburn, the trees & vegetation in general seem confined & stunted wanting that refreshing viridity which prevails elsewhere, but I suppose this is owing to the proximity of the sea. I scratched "J.T.P – K" on the back of one Timothy Jennings grave stone. We returned home by the Martello Towers & St. Leonard's, walked out by the sea shore in the evening & cut "J.P." on the lower part of the White Rock.

4 AUG
With Henderson to the noted fish ponds in the morning, which are encompassed with rows of thick tall trees & must be a fine shady walk upon a hot day, as it rained during our visit we could not enjoy the scenery so well, with my Father to Mrs. Wright's in the evening.

5 AUG
Walked on the East Hill before breakfast & attempted a sketch of All Saints' Church & part of the town, returned in the aftn. & finished it. I am happy to find my Father is rather better, we like our neat quiet lodgings very much.

6 AUG
To St. Leonards with my Father the fields way which being the longest much fatigued him, Mr Burton has opened a road communicating with the London High road, by means of which St. Leonards is approachable without passing through the old town. The Lodge built in the Gothic style took my fancy exceedingly. [*The gatehouse, spanning the road, was later owned and occupied for holidays by Sir Rider Haggard, the novelist.*] After dinner I met Henderson & bathed with him near the Martello towers.

7 AUG
With my Father to the fish market in the morning, there is abundance of fine fish here & skate is favourite with my Father & very plentiful. Bathed by myself in the aftn.

8 AUG

Walked on the Parade in the morning, & again in the evening when there was a grotesque looking young man dressed in cavalier Spanish fashion, playing the guitar & singing also very well. There were many opinions concerning who he might be & the ladies in particular were anxious to discover his name, by some it is reported that he is the son of Earl Stanhope who has undertaken to perform a round of the watering places in this disguise & to subsist, together with servant without asking alms. Whoever he may be he is certainly young and handsome with very superior & graceful manners. He resembles a troubadour of ancient days & has a good voice, he lives in the first style at one of the first hotels, he takes money when offered him but never asks for any. To all questions put to him as to his name he maintained a stubborn silence.

9 AUG

Walked with my Father up to the Castle then down the West Hill & so through the town home, he seemed much pleased with his walk. At night we applied a blister to his back in hopes of relieving the dreadful pain in his breast .

10 AUG

A wet morning, with my Father to Humphries in the morning and on the Parade in the evening. The gay, gallant incognito was there again.

11 AUG

Went early in the morning to the West Hill & made a sorry sketch of All Saints' church & the vicarage. This could be made a great scene of by a clever hand, went on the rocks fishing in the evening, caught several crabs & had them cooked.

12 AUG

To Mr. Humphries with my Father in the morning met Mr. Kingcombe near our cottage. He has come down to join Humphries in the newspaper. My Father intends to return on Sunday & will leave me for a time to live with Mr. Humphries.

13 AUG

Went to the Town Hall [*now the Hastings Museum*] with my Father to hear some cases. Mr. Humphries was brought up for striking his workman, he defended himself in a vehement manner & concluded by stating he would be justified in knocking the fellow's brains out if insulted in his own house! There was a general laugh against the little man.

14 AUG

Sketched the Castle from Pelham Cottage [*near Pelham Crescent, facing the sea*], the same our residence. To the coach office in the evening to book a seat in the stage.

15 AUG

Messrs. Humphries & Kingcombe, with the type founder & pressmaker, called on us in the morning. We went to Mrs. Humphries in the evening who lives in a little house above Wellington Square.

16 AUG, Sunday

Saw my Father safe off in the morning by the stage, took up my residence with Humphries at the *Chronicle* Office, High Street. Slept on my Father's easy chair.

17 AUG

In the office most of the day amusing myself with 'brevior short', 'long italic', etc.

18 AUG

Called upon Mrs. Wright in the morning, at home greater part of the day. No new bed!

19 AUG

To the Post Office in the morning, but no parcel or letter; also to Mr. Risby but nothing from my Father. This is very odd.

20 AUG

Walked to Battle and back (16 miles) after dinner for Mr. Kingcombe, but the person I sought had removed, on coming back I found my box, two letters from my Father, remittance etc. had arrived; he is yet very ill, Mrs. Kingcombe & family will come to Hastings next week.

21 AUG

Wrote to my Father in the Morning, & slept at Kingcombe's lodgings as he would be up all night.

22 AUG

Within doors most part of the day, my feet are much swelled.

23 AUG, Sunday

Took a walk towards Beachy Head in the forenoon. Mr. K. received a letter from my Father.

24 AUG

The 4th number of the *Hastings Literary Chronicle* came out to-day, & will I conclude from its bad sale, be the last. Blackguard Mick took it round to the subscribers.

25 AUG

Mrs. Kingcombe & family came down by the stage. I now take Mr. K's late lodgings, a great comfort.

26 AUG

Mr. and Mrs. Kingcombe paid Mrs. Wright a visit in the evening. She behaved as well to them as her prim, starch, stiff, old maidlike habits would allow. Oh thou ungracious Miss Cheese!

27 AUG

Mr. Underwood called in the morning, he has recently arrived from Brighton, and lodges in Wellington Square.

28 AUG

Mr. K. left Hastings for London in the evening. Mrs. K, George & self went part of the way with him.

29 AUG

Humphries is bringing out *Diplock's Guide*. He considers printing "dam hard work" & the neighbours have a knack of bawling out "another pint for the printer" so frequent are his libations of their potential beverage. His motto should be "Repetitur Libamen".

30 AUG, Sunday

Walked out with Mrs. Kingcombe & the family on the rocks picking up shells, etc. We continued along the sea shore as far as St Leonards.

31 AUG

Mr. Underwood left on his return to London by way of Brighton in the morning.

2 SEP

Went on the sands by the fish market in the afternoon. Saw one of Breede's brigs, coal laden from London, discharging cargo. She was hauled high & dry up on the Beach.

3 SEP

Went with George K. near St. Leonards after dinner, where we had a refreshing bathe.

4 SEP

With George all round the Castle, I determined to eclipse all the initials which disfigure the large flat rock near the Castle gate, I therefore cut a P eight inches long, 2 broad and 2 deep which will surely last as long as I shall. [*This rock remains in 1995, cut by innumerable initials*.]

5 SEP
Left Hastings in the afternoon for London. George walked 4 miles on the road with me, expecting the van to overtake me but it did not. After leaving Battle it became very dark & rained most unmercifully. I groped my way in the dark as well as I could, & discovered a small inn about 2½ miles from Battle, where I put up and had a comfortable bed.

6 SEP, Sunday
Arose at 6 o'clk & off directly on my journey, had breakfast at an inn four miles from Lamberhurst. While going through a toll gate a gentleman passed on horseback & one side of *my fine green surtout* caught in his spur at the moment & was sadly torn. This accident is singular, as occurring on a lonely road when he was the only traveller I had seen all the morning. To think we could not pass each other without damage to my piece of superfine. Plague take him!

On my arrival at the top of Lamberhurst Hill, a fine deer, closely pursued by a dog bounded by me with the velocity of lightening. Stayed & refreshed myself at Woodsgate, where the 4 Hastings stages met at one minute, then on to Tunbridge. Spied an old castle over the bridge but could not wait, proceeded on the road. It came on to rain heavily three miles from Sevenoaks, walked along with a gentleman into the town; he lent me an umbrella and pointed out the seven oaks. Put up at the Wheatsheaf intending to wait for the meal, but there were a party of young rascals swearing & gambling so profanely that I determined going on & put up at a neat little inn at Riverhead.

7 SEP
Up early in the morning & walked on within a mile of Farnboro' where I had an excellent breakfast, got my coat mended at Bromley Common, took a little beer at Bromley & then proceeded through Greenwich Road, Westminster & Oxford Street – HOME.

My Father very, very bad. My box arrived soon after me in the carrier Bridge's cart. Uncle & Lewis called. My Uncle appeared much pleased with my pedestrian feat.

8 SEP
In Uncle's chaise with my Father to Sir Astley Cooper [*consulting surgeon to Guy's Hospital*] & then to Dr. Wheelwright, called on Mr. Shackle with whom we dined. Emily & Eliza on a visit there, the latter returned in the gig & I walked home.

9 SEP
With my Uncle to the City in the gig, which I brought back to Kilburn. After this

I went to West End with my Father. On my return I drove cousins Betsy Pocock & Martha Bartlett to the Regent's Park and afterwards went with my father to Dr. Laing, who says he can certainly cure him. I left my Father at Westminster. Returning home though Hyde Park, a pretty air balloon descended close by me.

10 SEP
With my Uncle to the City. Brought back the chaise, & then attended a sale of some fruit trees at a nursery ground near Maida Hill, wishing to purchase some for my Uncle's garden. I was much disappointed when, on coming to the trees I wanted, the auctioneer Mr. Café informed he should sell nothing more as enough had been sold to pay the debts of the estate. Dined with my Uncle & walked to Paddington in the evening.

14 SEP
Walked to Charing Cross where my Mother & Uncle arrived in the chaise. I drove her to Brixton, then took my Father & Emma Underwood to Dulwich & Camberwell. Drove my Mother & baby home again in the evening.

17 SEP
Went to Fenchurch Street to meet my Father, then Guildhall, waited until 3 o'clk. I then walked to St. Bride's, met Samuel my cousin in Salisbury Square who questioned me concerning Hastings, etc., went again to Guildhall, but not seeing my Father returned home.

19 SEP
Walked to Paddington.... overtook cousin Betsy on the road & brought home a parcel for her.

20 SEP
My Mother went to Brixton early in the morning to see my Father....

22 SEP
Walked off early with Daniel my Uncle's groom to Stamford St. to get the gig, which was not finished. I then went to Dr. Laing & met my Parents there. Afterwards with them in a Hackney coach to St. Bride's. My Uncle very pleased to see Papa. We saw him safe in a Brixton stage - then came home.

23 SEP
Mr. Kingcombe to breakfast, himself & family have returned from Hastings he having dissolved partnership with Humphries.

24 SEP

Walked to Underwoods' early, Mr. Kingcombe there. He and I went out together to look for some quiet apartments for my Father as the least noise distracts him. After a long round we found a suitable place near Battersea Fields, here I left Kingcombe & came home over Vauxhall Bridge.

25 SEP

At home all day, arranging paths in the garden.

27 SEP

Walked over Vauxhall Bridge with my Uncle to see my Father. Walked from Underwoods to Kilburn in 1 hour & 20 minutes. I took a solitary walk in the fields after dinner.

28 SEP

Took my Father his easy coat and called on Lewis Pocock for some magazines....

30 SEP

My Mother left to meet Papa at Dr. Laing's in the morning, I attended on my Uncle's estate to see the men at their work. He is building a substantial wall round the garden on Greville Hill.

Chapter Eight

A Death in the Family

1 Oct, 1829

Breakfasted with my Uncle, and superintended the workmen for him all day. Went to Stapleton's to order more bricks

2 Oct

Took breakfast with my Uncle. I am in high favor with him – he much wishes me to be in his office & said he would ask Samuel again to-day. Attended his building all day.

3 Oct

To Paddington before breakfast for my Uncle. In the afternoon I went to see my Father & found him to my great grief much worse. He is sadly despondent himself and told me "he did not think he should live many days". On my return home I cautiously told my Mother how utterly hopeless our expectations of his recovery were, when she experienced a violent hysteric fit, but on coming to herself was remarkably calm. Almighty God! Thy ways are inscrutable, but thy will be done!

4 Oct

Walked to Brixton with Uncle, we were delighted to find my Father much better, nay even cheerful. Came back soon. Phoebe Underwood came in breathless at tea time saying my dear Father had been taken suddenly worse after we left him, and wished to see my Mother immediately. I directly informed my Uncle of this & went to Oxford Street & saw them in a Brixton stage.

5 Oct, Sunday

Rode to town with my Uncle & then with Lewis in the chaise to see my Father, who is no better. Mama yet remained with him; we called upon Mr. Taylor of Kennington, his present medical attendant. We then drove to Chelsea & I parted with him at Hyde Park corner.

6 Oct

Rode to St. Bride's Wharf, took lunch with my Uncle & then went to the Haymarket to meet my Mother. Weather very bad, rain & snow falling, alternately, I was wet through & waited ½ hour for her arrival. We went together to an upholsterer to procure an easy chair for my Father, after which I left her on the road to Brixton again, heavy fall of snow on my way home.

8 Oct

My Mother went to Brixton in the morning, my Father no better. He wished to be brought to Kilburn *that he may die in his own house.* Heavens, how terrible! The physicians are fearful to remove him on account of the large abscess in his breast, which would cause instant death, should it burst.

9 Oct

Walked to Charing Cross, where my Uncle and Mother in the gig overtook me. I then drove her to my Father who is no better, he wished to see Mr. Murrell & I went there with Mrs. Kingcombe. Then drove home for a pair of supports with the help of which my Father thought he could get up. Took the gig to St. Bride's & walked over, returned with my Mother at night.

10 Oct

James Magson called in the aftn. & I walked with him to Finchley along the new road cut from St. John's Wood. There is a beautifully situated old church almost obscured by the thick foliage of the surrounding trees. In the interim I found my Father had been brought home in an easy fly, much to the satisfaction of my Mother whose assiduities can be bestowed much better on him here. We went up to his old bedroom, the right hand front room, in the right hand bow, & he walked in freely; [*From that room he came not again alive. J.T. Pocock, 1835.*] Of his immediate danger he is perfectly sensible, for on bidding Mrs. Underwood farewell, who had been so very kind to him during his stay at her house, he said, "God bless you Mrs. Underwood, I shall seek a good place for you in the other world."

11 Oct

Our whole conversation dwelt upon my Father.

12 Oct, Sunday

In making my journal a/c in the evening my mind was much distressed with thinking upon poor Papa & I endeavoured to find relief in making a verse, but it is a very poor one –

> Father, they tell me thou art bad
>> And with sickness thou art sad,
> That soon thy pulse will cease to flow
>> And then be laid to rest below.
> All this fear'd, and to dispel
>> Those fears, I had recourse to tell
> That you were better and I hoped,

'Ere another month eloped,
To find gay Health return to thee
   In all her perils and luxury.
Frequent I wished, but wished in vain,
   For Health; she never came again.
And now to know that you must die,
   To know I wished by hopelessly;
To think on this, I sudden start,
   As if an arrow pierced my heart.
O cruel fate, that one so kind,
   Death will no longer leave behind.
Death! If thou wilt, so let it be,
   My Father leave and accept me.

13 OCT

Mr Lloyd of St Bartholomew's Hospital came in the morning. He ordered immediate bleeding to relieve the suffocating pain at the chest. My dear Father was in excruciating agony about sunset & walked about the room, then laid his head on the table &, uncovering his white shrunken arm, exclaimed, "Bleed me, bleed me." Miss Underwood & I went off to young Dr. Rogers who offered an excuse for not coming, shame to him.

14 OCT

To Oxford Street for medicine for my Father. Coming back I met Mrs. Wright to whom I addressed the usual question, "How do you do Madam"; she replied, "I do not know if I shall speak to you after the reception I have met with." She continued some invectives against my parents, which I parried, & also showed me a parcel in which she exultingly told me were some books of my late friend Josiah, which were intended for me but now I should not have them. I afterwards learned she had been to Kilburn when my Mother (considering her ill treatment to my poor Father at Hastings) sent the servant down to say she was engaged. Very properly too. I thought my Father's dim eyes glistened with pleasure when in reply to his expression of regret that I should have lost the books, I answered, I should have scorned to accept them from such hands.

16 OCT

My poor Father equally bad today.

18 OCT

At home all day with my Father. He is frequently seized with a sense of suffocation when attempting to lie down at which time he is compelled to jump out of bed & stand erect or he could not breathe.

19 OCT, Sunday

My Mother took an insect to Dr. Gardner, which my Father voided from his lungs or fancied so. I wrote a letter to my brother George at night.

20 OCT

To Islington, Hornsey & the Wharf with Uncle. Put George's letter in the St. Helena box at the East India House.

22 OCT

Rode to the City, called on Thomas Pocock [*a lawyer; second son of J.T. Pocock*], St. Bartholomew Close. A letter arrived from George to James Magson. My Father is rather more easy to-day but very melancholy.

25 OCT

My Father much worse to-day & sensible of approaching dissolution. In the afternoon he called us all in the room & bid us farewell individually. There were some of his favorite russet pippins on the table, & he divided them, giving half an apple to each child; this he adopted as a relief to the solemn scene. My Father was a strong-minded man, I never knew him to be overcome by his feelings until now; he had a rare and perfect command over all his passions until now; but this affecting scene was too much for him. He thought he would have gone through it with fortitude, but when it came to the eldest children, Emily & myself, for our share, he could no longer conceal his grief. Nature had her way & my Father covering his eyes with shrunken hands wept, bitterly wept, & we were equally moved. To me, and me only, he gave a whole apple & this I will keep for ever.

26 OCT

Called up in the night & ran to my Uncle, my Father's agony exceeded all description. When the worst paroxysms took place he suddenly jumped out of bed & then in the air nearly as high as the ceiling; next running to the window, he had it open & when he hoped his sufferings were over became better. In the intervals between these fits, he desired every knife, or instrument of any kind, to be taken out of his sight as he feared he might commit suicide so intense & unbearable was the feeling of being suffocated.

27 OCT

At home all day with my Father who is dreadfully bad, his strong constitution continues to baffle the disease he labours under.

28 OCT

Went to Harlesden Green to measure some land for my Father. My dear Father was very bad all day & Mrs. Kingcombe who sat up with him all night thought several times he was no more. My Uncle called in the morning when my Father was walking about the room in great agony, but with a firm step, on seeing his brother he exclaimed, "John for a brave man like me, who could lay my head on this table & have it cut off with all the ease in the world; to be strangled like a dog, & no human aid for me is *horrible*, horrible!"

After I went to bed my Mother called me up, to witness alas, suffering which no human aid could alleviate. Father then in broken accents was praying to God to relieve him by death, my Mother was kneeling on the floor, her hands upon a chair & praying also for his decease, she asked me imploringly to pray also that the Almighty should receive his spirit. I made an attempt but no, I could not pray for my beloved Father's death!

29 OCT

Mr Cowne the surgeon and Dr. Howship, whom my Mother called in yesterday, were in attendance to-day, went for medicines twice to Mr. Cowne's house, again at 11 p.m. for more of the opium pills which give my Father much relief.

30 OCT

Father expressed himself very much satisfied with Cowne the surgeon who was the first medical man to give him any relief. I was alone with him in the afternoon when he was sitting at the table and took out his will, broke the seal & added a memorandum, then resealed it & put it bye with great ease: he said to me "My dear boy, I do not hold out any delusive hopes of my recovery but this man has wrought Heaven upon me!" I was much alarmed at the increased rattling noise in his throat but he had experienced this many weeks.

31 OCT

I awoke at 7 o'clk & found my dear Father in his last moments. I addressed him & took hold of his clammy cold hand, but he heard me not, felt me not, sense & suffering had left him together. I then went to my Uncle & on my return met my sister Emily who told me the vital spark had flown, yes, the spirit of my Father had vacated its earthly tenement, to soar to a happier sphere, a home where sickness & sorrow are alike unknown!

Agreeable to his request an examination of his body took place in the afternoon by Dr. Howship & Mr. Cowne. It was discovered he laboured under two diseases, either of which would have terminated existence, he had aneurism of the aorta, the effusion of blood through the artery had cause the large pulsating tumour on the right hypochindrium. For this disease (unaccountable in its origin) there was no mortal remedy, he had also adhesion of the lungs to the sternum and ribs proceeding from active & ill treated inflammation of that organ at some distant period, this accounts for his paroxysms & sense of suffocation. In other respects he was sound & healthy. The physician gave it as his opinion that my father had a frame which promised longevity but for these diseases. My Father had the greatest dislike to remaining in bed throughout all his illness, & to this dislike he adhered with great tenacity, the day before his death, he walked freely about the room & sat at table, nay he even died sitting in his easy chair. Mr. and Mrs. Kingcombe who were present at the moment told us his last unconscious moments were perfectly calm & easy, & that with his last breath the abscess disappeared.

[*When the human mind is affected to the utmost extent with worldly grief, there is often a strange & kind intervention of Providence, by means of which we experience much comfort when we may have thought all consolation hopeless; and this was the case with my mother who on this trying occasion discovered more relief in the perusal of the Bible, than she could ever have supposed or anticipated.*

On the morning of my Father's decease, my Mother had been persuaded by Mrs. Kingcombe to take a little rest, which she stood in much need of, but did not retire until 2 or 3 oclk in the morning, my Father died a few hours afterwards, but she was not aware of this until 9 o'clk when she ran into the apartment, and seeing the corpse returned shocked & aghast to her own room. I speedily sought her & found her reading the Bible in bed, her looks were calm & resigned, & on my entering the room, she silently gave me her hand & pointed to the book.

I had gone there for the express purpose of consoling my Mother by beseeching her to be resigned to the will of God, yet when I entered the room, I was dumb, I could not speak; & yet our feelings assimilated so well that there was no need of words to express the sentiments of the heart; there is a communion of the soul which needs not the mouth to interpret, & the communion or coalition is conversable though the eyes. My Mother looked on me, & I gazed on her, & when she feelingly pressed my hand, which pressure was returned, the feelings of both were better & more eloquently expressed & felt, that the most voluable & fluent language could designate; she had lost her husband & supporter and of course looked upon me, being her eldest son at home as her future defender & prop. I had lost a kind & indulgent father, and in gratitude for his past benefits in common with great affection for my Mother, made me anxious to do all in my power to relieve her; our grief flowed from one common source. John Pocock, 1835.]

2 Nov

At home all day writing letters to some of our friends acquainting them with our loss.

4 Nov

At home all day. Miss Underwood is kindly assisting to make up the mourning dresses for my Mother & Sister.

9 Nov

Mrs Kingcombe went to Mrs. Chappell [*probably the wife of Samuel Chappell, now living in Greville Place*] who is kindly making up some of the mourning dresses.

10 NOV

Went to Captain Murray, Soho Square, & left a letter for my brother George, acquainting him with our death Father's death.

11 NOV

Walked to town then to St. Bride's, saw Mr. Murrell, who has to conduct the funeral.

12 NOV

Early in the morning I went to Paddington for my Uncle & again for my Mother, Mr. Murrell came at ½ past 11, Mr. & Mrs. Underwood soon after, my Uncle & cousins Samuel & Lewis & Mr. Holmes. At ¼ before 2 o'clk the procession consisting of a hearse & mourning coach moved towards St. Johns Wood Chapel. My Uncle, Cousins, Messrs. Underwood & Holmes attended only as mourners, but my friends James Magson & William Robinson were at the grave. The clergyman, a young gentleman, preached the beautiful service for the dead in a clear & impressive manner. I was very unwell in going up the walk of the churchyard, but this did not arise from grief. The beloved remains of my dear Father were interred in the grave No. 4b, Letter T, & very near the resting place of Joanne Southcote, the noted imposter. I cannot say I felt very much until the sexton threw the earth upon the hollow sounding coffin, when the preacher said "ashes to ashes, dust to dust" then indeed I felt the sound strike as it were in my inmost heart. I left my friends Magson & Robinson by the grave & returned in the coach, my cousins went home soon but my Uncle and friends remained to tea.

[*My Father! Blessings on the name; for he was indeed to me a father in the unlimited acceptance of that term; what tho' his faults and frailties were numerous, did not the many virtues he professed more than counterbalance them all? I am inclined to think his errors are rather to be placed to account of the manner he was brought up and allowed to spend his younger days, than to any natural inclination or tendency to vice. It was his misfortune to be the favourite child with his father and mother, and on this account any baneful whim or caprice he indulged in was entirely overlooked by his overfond parents.*

He was born in the pleasant village of Chiswick about the year 1777 where his father like himself was a great speculator in building. He was brought up as a land surveyor, and from his infancy was ever in the society of builders, and amongst bricks and mortar. He mixed freely with the gay youth of the metropolis during his 'teens, especially the reigning belles and beaux of Islington and its vicinity when he was a subscriber to almost every ballroom, assembly or concert. He belonged to a noted Whist Club; at the game of whist he was perhaps one of the best players extant. Indeed among the circle in which he moved he was known as an established 'man of ton'. He continued his gallant dissipated career until his marriage, when his talents in his profession speedily brought him wealth, still he managed to live up to his income, and never for a moment thought of saving anything.

At the time of my birth [1814] he was perhaps in the zenith of his glory. He then lived in Leadenhall Street where I was born and had a second establishment in Fenchurch Street; but the City it would seem was not fashionable enough for his extended views and accordingly he took a large and splendid house in New Bond Street. At this time he was in the constant habit of giving extensive parties which were well attended by a circle of Friends....

As far back as I can well remember, we lived in Windsor Terrace, City Road and from there removed to Ivy Lane, Hoxton, where he purchased an estate and built about half the street as it now stands; from whence we removed to the fine and excellent estate of Kilburn, at the site of the old Priory. This was certainly one of the best speculations he ever made....the mansions he built sold as fast as they were finished. He ... might have done very well but for the encroachment of Col. Howard [probably the Hon. Fulke Greville Howard], who owned the adjoining Hilly Field Estate, and Mr. T. H. Mortimer, his solicitor; the latter continually advanced him sums of money at a high interest on security, which completely fettered his estate.

When we lived in the corner house in the Priory, I remember well he was still in affluent circumstances. He then kept three clerks.... many household servants, a house and gig and one of the finest teams of horses for miles around; let me see, there was fat Punch and Bull and Lobster and the black horse who lost his sight and whom Punch used to lead about the fields... But gradually his finances became impoverished, and his remaining land fettered beyond recovery. Then commenced his lamentable illness which put a stop to any pecuniary benefits arising from employment in his profession, then his friends fell off and deserted him, then his creditors became clamorous and involved him in continual difficulties; then Mortimer, like a mercenary man, refused him further assistance. My father notwithstanding had considerable innate pride and perhaps felt what Shakespear has so strongly expressed in words: 'The soul and body rive not more at parting than greatness going off', for he continued as far as laid in his power to support appearances and lived to the day of his death in the best and largest house in the Priory - a perfect triumph of architecture, and one of his own design, built expressly for himself. This house excited the envy of many of our neighbours. How well is that beautiful mansion pictured in my memory, how clearly do I view with my 'mind's eye' its two bold front bows, and the three elegant arches thrown across from the house to the stable, how clearly do I see the semicircular drive up to the front door – and now methinks I peep through the middle arch and look at the large and luxurious garden behind full of choice fruit trees and vegetables. Yes & there are the three lofty elms too, the pride of my Father, & my delight when they afforded so excellent a swing, aye, all is imprinted on "memory's seat" in colours too strong to be effaced, but enough of this, his house & garden are now in other hands, other children now traverse my nursery, other boys climb the trees, to affright the poor winged inhabitants, and other youngsters devour his favorite russet pippins & spoil the carefully nailed wall fruit trees.

In memory my Father was a perfect gentleman, affable, pliant & polite, his extensive intercourse with superior society had given him a polished & pleasing demeanour, he was liberal to a fault, gay thoughtless & imprudent, in early life he had contracted baneful, convivial habits which were never effaced until his illness assumed so alarming a shape as to prevent the continuance of them.

My Father, I am sorry to say, was never religious until his last days, when I have reason to hope and believe he became a true penitent. He was latterly continually lost in conflicting thoughtfulness and if those thoughts could be analysed I am persuaded they would prove the rumination upon a life mis-spent when, too late, he saw the usefulness of the saving principle so well adopted by my Uncle in the days of his youth. He saw when too late that the same principle caused my Uncle to be in the possession of a handsome fortune, his children all well provided for, himself enjoying the sweets after a life of laborious perseverance – when my Father who had better opportunities of gaining wealth was dying in poverty with a troop of unprovided children around his deathbed.

My Father professed too much of the milk of human nature to thrive permanently amongst the degenerate race of beings who now inhabit the world, for he was constantly the prey of sharpers who involved him in difficulties, yet his kind forgiving heart would allow him to think no more of these when the discomfiture produced by them had passed away. The greatest rascal of this class my Father ever became entangled with was John Bewley. I commit the name to paper with instinctive horror; how a man like my Father having so much experience of the world & of "men and manners" could have become the repeated dupe of this consummate villain is beyond my comprehension to fathom, he seemed to possess a supernatural power over him, quite unaccountable, which neither the prudent advice of my Mother nor the counsel of his own reason could overturn.

I have said my Father had been deserted by a host of friends who changed according to the change in his fortunes. In justice, however, to some of his old acquaintances, who continued the same in wealth and in poverty, I register with pleasure the names of these families: the Underwoods, Gurneys, Kingcombes, Shackles, Holmes, Rogers, Milner and last but not least - my Uncle - their friendship continued the same.

One fault, in justice to my Uncle, I must register against my parents. In my Father's 'bright day of glory and power' , my father courted not his acquaintance; then, he was not on so intimate terms as when he needed his assistance – and how did my uncle return the treatment? By heaping every comfort and blessing on him during his sickness and by supporting and cherishing his helpless widow and fatherless children in his decease! You, my kind and generous Uncle, are no more on this earth – accept the affectionate thanks from the son of your brother on whom you heaped so many generosities.

And how can I note my Mother's Goodness? To name it in two forcible words, she behaved, under these circumstances as a Woman and a Wife! – for her devotedness as Shakespear has it, 'Altered not, as it alteration found.' John Pocock, 1835.]

Chapter Nine

Journey to the Cape

17 NOV, 1829

To St. Bride's with my Uncle in the chaise, then walked to Mr. Holmes to enquire concerning the New Swan River [*Western Australia*] as my Uncle thinks of me going out there with a Mr. Carter, surgeon, & a friend of his. Mr. H. gives very flattering accounts of the place.

19 NOV

To St. Bride's with my Uncle. Went to 26 Stamford Street, then to 75 where Mr. C. had removed. Saw Mrs. C. who said she believed Mr. C. had engaged with everyone he had intended taking out with him.

24 NOV

To Mr. Carter with my Uncle. He asks £50 premium & wishes me to be bound for 5 or 6 years to him without which indenture I should not be an eligible candidate for the College of Surgeons.

25 NOV

With my Uncle to Mr. Carter where he left me & I went with him to St. Katherine's Dock, where the vessel is loading in which he has taken his passage, the *Medina* of 600 tons, Walter Pace Commander. We went over his cabin which is spacious & well fitted up, & has a piano forte, etc. Returned & had dinner with him & Mrs. Carter, they treated me very kindly.

26 NOV

With Mr. Carter all the morning. Wrote out an agreement for him & a list of medicines contained in the ship's chest. Stayed dinner & called at St. Bride's on my way home.

27 NOV

My Uncle concluded with Mr. Carter about taking me, I remained with Mr. C. all day & walked home in the evening.

28 NOV

Went early to Dod & Son, Mark Lane, Ship Agents for samples of spirit for Mr.

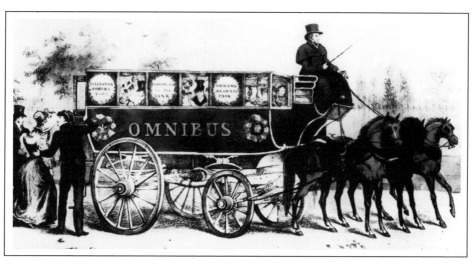

26. *George Shillibeer's omnibus, introduced on the New Road (today's Marylebone-Euston-Pentonville Roads) and City Road in 1829.*

C. and then with him to the *Medina* when he engaged my berth, returned home after dinner.

30 NOV, Monday
To Mr Carew, Capt Murray and with my mother to Mr Carter, then to Shackles where we remained dinner. Rode home in a Paddington omnibus.
[*George Shillibeer had begun the first London omnibus service in July of this year. Drawn by three horses abreast, the bus carried 22 passengers, inside only. It ran from the Bank to the Yorkshire Stingo in Marylebone. The fare was 1/- or 6d for half the way, with the use of a newspaper free.*]

2 DEC
To Stamford Street early & then with Mr. C. to the Docks, the *Medina* seems in a state of forwardness & is to sail on the 10th. I bought a few water colors on my way home.

3 DEC
Met Lewis in the New Road. We took a boat to London Bridge and afterwards rode in a *stagedickey* from the Elephant and Castle to the Underwoods.

4 DEC
Went to a sale at Westminster with Mr. C. & brought home some books for him.

5 DEC
With my Uncle to Bankside in the chaise, then walked homewards.

7 DEC

To the Docks with Mr. Carter arranging his cabin etc. & after dinner I walked home over Waterloo Bridge.

  To-ing and fro-ing to Carter & the Docks & saying farewell to friends.

8 DEC

With Uncle to Marylebone in a gig. Met Henderson going down to see me as he is about sailing as midshipman in H.E.S. [*Honourable East India Company's Ship*] *Thomas Coutts*. Walked back to Maida Hill. I went to Gurneys, they are about removing to Judd Street. I then went to Mr. Carter and to the Docks. Called at St. Bride's after dinner and rode home with my Uncle.

9 DEC

To the City with my Uncle in the chaise, then walked to Limehouse. Mr. Holmes being out, I went on to Poplar and on my return dined with Mr. H., who went with me to the Docks over the *Medina*. Called at the Wharf and Gurney's. On my return found Tom and Fred and James Magson there; spent a pleasant evening.

10 DEC

Rode from Maida Hill to Fleet Market in one of St Alban's long-stages with my Mother; we were terribly jolted over the stones. Then went to Mr. Carter with her, who accompanied us to the Docks with Mrs. C. On our return we stayed dinner, after which walked home.

12 DEC

On arrival Mrs C. sent me to Greenwich, I rode there in the four horse white omnibus. Walked home called at Uncle's when Lewis made me a present of a handsome fowling piece, he showed me how to load it & Betsy, Martha and myself each fired it off on the steps. At ½ past 11 a.m. I reached my 15th year.

13 DEC, Sunday

Shot a sparrow in the morning, what game! Walked out with Robinson in the afternoon in the fields towards Kensal Green with my gun on shoulder, sportsmanlike, saw no birds. I went with my mother to Dr. Rogers in the evening and bid the family farewell.

14 DEC

With Uncle to Paddington in the gig. He was fearful to go in the dense fog & so sent me back with the vehicle to Kilburn but told me to bring it on to the City if the weather cleared up. I soon set off again regardless of the fog & slashed through the old journey in fine style. Took up Mrs. Dickinson on the road & set her down at her home in Bond Street. My Uncle was much pleased when he found me arrive safe at the Wharf in weather which he dared not drive through.... Samuel generously gave me a handsome new silver hunter watch & Lewis a large bag full of books. Bought a handsome lock for my journal & some writing paper, going home. I may well call this collecting day.

15 DEC
In the morning went to Stamford Street, my boxes arrived in the Kilburn Carrier's cart.

16 DEC
At home all the morning. Walked to Mr. Bilney in the afternoon, gun in hand; met my old drawing master, Mr. Weeden, in the lane.

17 DEC
With my Uncle to the Wharf and then to Mr. Carter, where we signed, sealed and delivered my Article of Apprenticeship, binding me for the term of six years from the 8th instant, to learn "the art and mystery" of a Surgeon Apothecary and Accoucheur in consideration of a sum of £50 premium and £12 outfit, which sum of £62 my Uncle gave him a check for.

18 DEC
With my Mother to Paddington, then Mr. Carter's and on to the Docks, where I found him, returning dined at the Wharf and took tea with Lewis and Samuel.

20 DEC
Walked with my Uncle to see Mr. Kennedy and viewed his valuable collection of pictures. [*Some of John Kennedy's collection of paintings at Burton Crescent can be seen in the illustration on the jacket and on the title pages.*] Returning, Lewis P. and Henry Kennedy overtook us. My Uncle invited me to dine with him; the Bartletts, Mr. Lawrence, who is shortly to marry Betsy, Samuel, etc., were there. [*Betsy did not marry Mr. Lawrence, but became Mrs. Thomas Vacher.*] We had a regular Christmas Day dinner. My Uncle and I went part of the way home with the guests. Martha, my cousin, slipped ½ sovereign in my hand and insisted on my acceptance of it.

21 DEC
To Stamford Street & the Docks with Mr. Carter, *Medina* is to sail on 19th inst. With Mr. C. to St. Bartholomew's Hospital – in the Aldersgate Street dissecting room over the Museum saw Thurtle's skull and Bellingham's there. [*John Thurtell, the son of a Mayor of Norwich, had been a prize-fighter and been hanged for murder in 1824; John Bellingham had been hanged for the assassination of Spencer Perceval, the Prime Minister, at the House of Commons in 1812.*] Subjects were very scarce & the disjointed members were laying on the dissecting tables with the tickets of price of each affixed. Lewis took tea with us & afterwards attended the lecturing Theatre of the Hospital. Mr. Lawrence the eminent surgeon treated in Eresipelas

& Nettlerash. Left Mr. C. & Lewis soon after in Smithfield, rode from the Angel [*probably the Angel Inn, Holborn*] in an omnibus.

23 Dec

With Mr. Carter to the Docks, stayed dinner, saw Mr. Rowland Wimburn, a Chancery Solicitor and Mrs. Carter's father; he seems a kind & good old gentleman, took tea with my cousins at St. Bride's.... Betsy gave me a drawing book.

24 Dec

With Mr. Carter to the docks, finally arranging his cabin, returned home & called upon Uncle afterwards.

25 Dec

At home all the morning, had a plentiful Christmas dinner & played at snap-dragon afterwards. The children went to Chapel.

26 Dec

Went to Mr. Carter early & took two fowling pieces to the Docks for him. Ship had removed and was filling water. Met Lewis in Paternoster Row, he has purchased me 1 cwt. of shot, had tea with him & Samuel. James Magson came in the evening.

27 Dec, Sunday

Snow thick on the ground.

28 Dec

On arrival in Stamford Street, I went to Greenwich by stage, having a bad cold, my Uncle requested my staying with him all night. We went together to Upper Thames St. to an ironmonger store as he is going to send a small investment of cutlery for my disposal. We then rode in an omnibus to the Angel Inn & there met my mother & Mrs Shackle. Saw the former on to the Kilburn stage & went home with the latter who presented a seal & watch guard to me.

29 Dec

We rode in a hackney coach to the Docks to embark, calling for my shot on the way. James Magson was on board, at 2 o'clk we swung out of Dock, a steamer lying in the river to take us in tow. Left my Mother on the drawbridge with her brother. When we were clear, the dockmen & all the crowd gave us a deafening hip hip hurra, three repeated which was repeated by all our men, we then went slowly down the River. Samuel & Batcock passed us in one of my Uncle's barges, deeply laden, soon after the pipes of the Steamer froze & we were compelled to anchor alongside a collier. At this time Mr. Carter was called to James Lloyd, a passenger, who was dying; we put him in a bath but he immediately expired. This is making a bad beginning. The cold to-day is most intense & the River full of floating ice; could not keep myself warm by any means.

30 DEC

Arose at 7 o'clk after a restless night, went on deck. The weather dreadfully cold, at 2 p.m. a fresh steamer came and after much ado with the starboard and larboard warps alternately, took us safely down to Gravesend where we anchored at 7 o'clk. No provisions being yet given by the ship, we are badly off and the cold weather adds to our misery.

31 DEC

On shore in the morning with Mr. C. & Savory. Gravesend is as ugly, straggly, ill-built kind of town as I could wish to see. We took some warm ale at an Hotel and I then mounted a London Stage and stopped at Greenwich, went also to the Court of Requests [*a court for the recovery of small debts*]. I then rode to town, calling at the Wharf, walked to the end of Gray's Inn Lane & then took omnibus to Paddington, on my way home. My dear Mother and all the children were at home. Saw Lewis, Betsy and Martha Bartlett after tea. I walked with the former to Paddington, a beautiful moonlight night, which seemed the more so to me as it was the last of my spending at home. On my return Mrs. Kingcombe was at our house and sadly annoyed us with her presence as I wished to talk exclusively to Mama being the only opportunity I may ever have again. My Mother wished her at old Scratch and I ditto; slept with dear little Lewis who cuddled me, he said, for the last time.

1 JAN, 1830

Took breakfast with Betsy, Martha & Lewis, wished the ladies farewell & then came to take my final leave of my Mother & the dear children. I kissed them severally & ran into the front garden. My cousin Lewis was waiting in the gig for me, however, I ran back again to give my poor Mother an extra kiss; she was crying bitterly but I consoled her by the prospects of a happy meeting hereafter. I then tore myself away from them & ran to the gate, just as the house was closing from my view, little Maria ran out & cried "Goodbye John". These were the last words I heard, another minute we were driving at a fine rate to the metropolis. I looked back upon Kilburn as long as I could catch a glimpse of the place and I never knew Kilburn look so lovely before.

On arrival at the Wharf I saw my Uncle, he gave me £2.10.0. to furnish my waistcoat pocket with. I then parted with them & got a coal heaver to carry my box of goods with me to the Elephant & Castle, where I took stage to Greenwood's, got Mr. Carter's money, then went to Turnpike for the Gravesend stage which came up full. Waited an hour shivering in the cold for another, on which I rode to Gravesend, & got safely on board at 6 o'clock, put my box of goods at the end of my berth; to bed soon after.

2 JAN

Received a kind letter from my cousin Lewis, who wishes me to write every opportunity. Mr. Carter went to London in the morning, we are getting rather more comfortable now; the exciseman is still on board.

3 JAN

James Magson came in the morning & brought my 3rd vol. of *The Casket*; it is very kind of him being at his own expense. He seemed particularly low spirited & left by the steamer in the aftn. Mr. C. returned and I went with him to see him prepare some medicines, which I shall soon have to do myself.

4 JAN

Foggy day preventing the shore being seen by us. Mr. C. bled a Mrs Pollyblank in the morning. The process appears simple & easy.

5 JAN

Mr. C. explained to me the difference between the crassamentum & serum of the blood drawn yesterday, also when buffy & cupped, showing existing inflammation etc. Johnson went on shore & brought me a letter from my Mother: all well at home.

6 JAN

We left Gravesend at 11 a.m. but anchored below waiting for the Captain who soon came & we set sail with a fair breeze, proceeding rapidly. At 6 pm., we passed the Nore light & about 9 cast anchor as the pilot considered it unsafe to go on further by night.

7 JAN

On heaving in cable at daybreak it was discovered we had lost one of our best bower anchors, we then set sail with a fine strong breeze & some of the passengers began what is called 'casting accounts' & 'discharging the bill'; or 'heaving the cat'. I laughed at the squeamish ones finely & kept on deck quite well. Mr. & Mrs. Carter were completely laid up. At 2 o'clock we were in the Down's where we hove to about ½ an hour & took on a Deal pilot. We then proceeded with great rapidity along the Channel, Dover looked very pretty from the water. I felt a little nausea in the evening & ran on deck to seek fresh air, when I was met by a dirty devil boy, Sam, who pushed a lump of fat pork in my mouth appended to a string. This completed the catastrophe & I crawled below to my 'bunk' very queer, very queer.

8 JAN

Arose early in the morning & ate a hearty breakfast in defiance of sea sickness. Wind shifted a little & we were tacking all day. Chartres a seaman is ill of ague, Mr. C. is giving him bark [*quinine*]. I was awoke at midnight by our cable which was let go to bring the ship up off Portsmouth.

9 JAN

Found in the morning that we had cast anchor about 3 miles from Portsmouth and 1½ miles from the Isle of Wight. Several of the passengers went ashore. Mr. Hayman, sole owner, came aboard; he did not relish the loss of the anchor which was re-supplied. I wrote two letters one for my mother & one for Lewis which I gave Mr. Manning to post for me.

10 JAN, Sunday

Shipped all our passengers & should have sailed had the wind proved fair.

11 JAN

Left Portsmouth about 2 oclk p.m. when the owner left us and also the pilot soon after we had passed the Warner Buoy, after clearing the Isle of Wight. I soon lost sight, perhaps for ever, of my native land. "The night was drear and dark" & we were going 7 knots through the water. I was dreadfully sick in the evening.

12 JAN

Very ill all day and the other passengers also laid up.

13 JAN

Saw Mr. Carter in the morning, who like myself remains very sick. The old lady creates most confoundedly.

14 JAN

Still very sick and have eaten nothing but a piece or two of gingerbread these three days past. Got up for a short time in the afternoon, the sea looks awefully *blue* or purple like ourselves. We left the Bay of Biscay in the evening proceeding rapidly on.

15 JAN

Felt rather better, went to Mr. Carter's cabin & saw Mrs. C. who feels the motion of the vessel as much as ourselves. A Mrs Byers took it into her head to go into Hysterics in the afternoon.

27 & 28. John Pocock's sea chest, now belonging to his brother's great-grandson, Professor John Pocock of Baltimore, Maryland, USA.

16 JAN

Off the coast of Spain, foul wind, a homeward bound brig passed near us but not within hail. Went with Howell to the Steward's pantry who served out our provisions.

17 JAN

Fine calm day, the wind unfair, a man named Cooper is affected by *chymanch tonsillaris.*

18 JAN

With Mr. C. to his cabin when I took various medicines to various folks, the wind continues 'in our teeth' as the sailors say.

19 JAN

Mr. C. bled Cooper until fainting at his usual hour of visiting patients in the morning; we had squally weather at night & the long boat was nearly lost having broken from its cleats.

20 JAN

Took medicines from Mrs. Hammond, Cooper alias 'Jack you're wanted' and the cook Curtis who is dangerously ill with quinsy. The rascally Jack Tars call me 'bloody boy' which is sadly derogative to my important situation as *doctor's mate!* Really, this epithet is an invasion upon my *aetum cum dignitate.* Wind is more favourable.

21 JAN

Weather getting comfortably warm, but much sickness prevails in the ship owing to the late cold weather.

22 JAN

Made considerable progress to-day being in N Lat 37 degrees Long 13 W. The Steward's mate or 'Cuddy boy John' and Cooper's brother had sore throats.

24 JAN, Sunday

Mrs Carter read prayers in her cabin in the morning. We continue with favourable winds.

25 JAN

Dressed the cuddy boy's neck, cook's leg etc: in the morning, our mess take it in turns to wash up the plates and dishes after all hands, and this week it comes to my turn; how my sisters would laugh to see me with sleeves tucked up after such a set of greasy knaves.

26 Jan

With Mr. C. to his patients, the cook or 'doctor' as the seamen call him is much better. I was standing on the forecastle in the afternoon looking on 'the sea the mighty sea' when a gust of wind very impolitely took my leather cap overboard.

27 Jan

Mrs Hammond very ill, expecting her accouchement. We are going on with a fair breeze at the rate of 8 knots.

29 Jan

Attended to the Steward, his mate and others in the morning. I exchanged my rum for vinegar as the 'junk' is rather wanting in flavour and I cannot eat the pork.

30 Jan

Fine day fair wind in N Lat 25" 50". I applied a *fomentation* of camomile flowers and poppy heads to Gilby's leg, he has rheumatic gout and found much relief from the application.

31 Jan

We had a good Sunday dinner to-day

1 Feb

Mr. C. gave me a long prescription to translate which I did with the help of Fearless. A large shark with six pilot fish in attendance was seen from the poop and a bait laid for him which he took but succeeded in getting away with damage to his mouth; two spermacette whales were seen spouting.

2 Feb

A dead calm all day. In the evening a dying pig was thrown overboard on my fiat of his being incurable.

3 Feb

Becalmed still got a comfortable bucket bath in the forecastle before breakfast.

4 Feb

Mr. C. called me in a hurry in the morning, the steps being away I climbed up the hatchway and had my legs pulled and picked by the iron-fingered sailors. A fine breeze came up in the afternoon.

5 Feb

The Cape de Verde in sight all day, one of them Buona Vista which we passed close by has a very majestic appearance. Mrs. Carter took a good sketch of it and I made *an attempt*.

6 FEB
Fine fair breeze, all sail set, made up a whole lot of calomel pills *cum Ext. Colocos Compos.*

8 FEB
Mr. C. gave me a lancet (one of my own) and promised I should bleed first opportunity, also two prescriptions to translate,

9 FEB
Chartres hurt his hand very severely while drawing up water. Mr. C. applied strips of plaster and lint to the wound.

10 FEB
A small shark only 3 feet in length was caught by Mr. Lemontin; he had but one row of teeth. Much quarrelling among the passengers in the evening, and one between Fearless and Nash the 3rd mate came to blows. Sargeant and the Captain parted them and Nash was ordered in to the poop for interfering with the passengers, there was also much wrangling amongst the cabin passengers and fighting ensued, many were drunk.

11 FEB
Becalmed, the intensity of the heat hardly bearable. Savory, Venn and Bailey were quarrelling all the evening. I slept on deck and could hardly breathe below. At 8 bells (midnight) I heard the report of a pistol and ran below to ascertain the cause, and found Savory with the doctor and Cowcher his head bleeding profusely from a pistol wound immediately behind his ear. He had been teasing Mr. Venn who acted up to his promise of shooting him if he continued his annoyance. The ball was not extracted owing to prevalence of fever, etc. Venn was ordered a prisoner in the poop by the Captain.

12 FEB
Saw Savory in the morning who is quite sensible, the ball does not appear to have affected his brains. Query, Has he any? A fine bark was seen on the larboard quarter all the morning making for us, at 4 oclk she came alongside and proved to be a Falmouth Packet out *30 days* bound to Brazil, the Captain was a degree out in his reckoning, she shot ahead of us (in ballast trim).

13 FEB
Becalmed all day, tasted some baked shark at dinner time which is none so bad. Mr Benningfield's child has the typhus fever.

14 Feb

A heavy refreshing rain continued all the morning when sails etc. were spread to catch it. The sailors all on deck taking advantage of it to wash their clothes.

15 Feb

Mr. Benningfield's child is much worse to-day.

16 Feb

With Mr. Benningfield's child all day who was in *articula mortis*. He occasionally rallied until 8 o'clk when, perceiving a change I sent Mrs. Westcott up to its father and on their return the child was dead. Mr. B. became like a madman at his loss and I remained up with him during the night applying restoratives.

17 Feb

The funeral of the child took place in the morning in the following manner, the coffin is placed on a hatch with the union jack over it. When the Captain came to read the usual sea service with a black velvet cap on his head, all the crew were ordered aft to witness the ceremony. At a signal given by the Captain the end of the hatch is tilted up when the coffin slides into the sea. Mr. B. was brought on deck insensible and remained so all day. We crossed the line at 6 o'clk in the evening, but owing to circumstances the shaving is postponed until to-morrow.

18 Feb

Preparations were made all the morning for the grand shaving match which began about 10 o'clk as follows, Neptune Smith disguised with long white hair literally concealing his face and one of the sailors dressed up as a woman, were placed in the lady's hoisting chair transfixed upon the carriage of one of the guns, and drawn by 4 sea dogs (4 apprentices) painted red and black all over; and two disguised attendants on each side, followed by the high constable, two shavers, Judge, tub assistants and 4 officers to catch the people. The procession came out from behind a curtain set before the galley.

It was so admirably arranged that even the Captain did not know his own crew, they were drawn in style up to the cuddy door at which the high constable knocked with his wand and demanded the Captain. Upon his appearance Neptune in an authorative tone, hailed the ship and desired to know the Captain's name, where she came from, her days passage etc. which he pretended to note in his register, at the same time he requested the Captain go near the car as his wife's hair was very wet, for his dogs had pulled them very fast through the water. He then desired for a list of the passengers, which was given to the high sherriff. He next ordered out the grog bottle and regaled his spouse in a loving manner with same, then whistling to the dogs with a boatswain's whistle, they were drawn completely round the ship to the place of action, the starboard quarter deck near the mainmast.

All the passengers were now ordered below who did not choose to be shaved and battened down. Many were cowardly enough to go down but the cabin passengers were allowed to witness the ceremony from the poop in forfeiture of a bottle of rum each. The large wash deck tub, filled with salt water and a sliding piece of wood across was put in readiness the shavers on each side. It appears Walter my friend (the Captain's son) and "the d----d doctor's mate Pocock" were predestined for extra punishment. Walter stood No. 1 and he was taken by the Constable blindfolded and then placed on the cross bar of wood, a mixture of tar, fat and other filth was then dashed over his face, and afterwards scraped by two blunt razors of enormous size made from an iron hoof by the carpenter, during which operation the seat was dexterously slipped away, when in he soused over head and heels, and was kindly kept under by the officers a long time. On getting free three or four buckets of water met him cooly in the face, and also a few thrown from the main top.

I stood No. 4 on the list and was treated even worse than Walter by concensus of Neptune when he heard the culprit was a young doctor, for on opening my mouth the brutal brush was pushed in. I could not get the taste out of my mouth all day. The shaving lasted above 2 hours and the crew were allowed the remainder of the day to drink out. Nash took the wheel.

It was altogether conducted excellently, I gave my day's grog for the largest of the two brutal razors as a curiosity to send home.

19 FEB
Being in the South West Trades we are going much out of our track. Helped Mr. C. to dress Savory's wound in the morning.

20 FEB
Hardacre's two children are ill, I made up and administered some medicine for both.

21 FEB, Sunday
Mrs. C. read prayers as usual. Mr. Carter bled Capt. Pearce's servant.

22 FEB
Squally weather all day. S. Lat 2° 36'.

23 FEB
S. Lat 12 M 4° 8'. Mrs. Hammond was delivered of a still born child in the evening.

24 FEB
Made up 12 dozen pills in the morning. S. Lat 6° 46' running fast down towards the Southward and Westward.

29. Bound for the Cape. First-class passengers on quarterdeck, in 1819.

25 Feb
Had a bucket bath with Walter in the morning, dressed Mr. Nash's finger.

26 Feb
Saw a vessel right ahead on the horizon at day break, wind fresh. We soon joined fast upon her and at 11 o'clk were alongside. She was a ketch ship-rigged and hoisted Genoese colors, stated herself from Genoa bound for Brazil. She dropped astern directly.

27 Feb
Fresh breeze all day, in the cradle in the bowsprit in the aftn, reading, this is my favourite place, the only solitary one on board.

28 Feb, Sunday
Prayers as usual. Mr. C. gave me a number of *The Lancet* to read and I found it very interesting.

1 Mar
Up at day break when a very heavy squall rose. I assisted them to shorten sail, spiniker, main topsail, jib, top-gallants etc. were furled.

2 MAR

Pritchard came on the list today having inoculated himself with a cowhide. Meredith fell down to fore-hatch at 11 p.m. and was bled in consequence.

3 MAR

Trinidad Islands in sight all the afternoon, they were first seen by Daly. We were much out in Longitude.

4 MAR

Strong breese all day S Lat 26° 46'. Reading most of the day.

5 MAR

A dead calm, the sails flapping dismally to the mast. Green drunk, Gilby and Laker fighting p.m. when the Captain parted them.

6 MAR

Becalmed, made up a quantity of medicines for our patients.

7 MAR

A fine serene day. Going 4 knots through the water, about ½ past 4 pm while reading below, I heard a cry "man overboard" and on running up, I saw a man's head above water and another person swimming up to it about ½ a mile astern. I was then informed that Green who was drunk, had jumped overboard for a swim, and that March who was at the helm when this took place, gallantly jumped after him. The ship was put all aback as soon as possible, and the gig lowered, manned by 4 hands at this time. March had hold of the man's hair and treading the water, was calling lustily for the boat which reached them in about 10 minutes (although the time seem much more to all of us who were waiting the result with breathless anxiety). They got Green safe in the boat and were beginning to pull for the ship when we heard them call for the other boat as the one they were in was sinking fast, which proved to be the case. The cutter was then lowered with 6 hands, but before she could come up with them, we saw the boat sink and then turned bottom upwards. Fortunately, they could all of them swim. At the time to our dismay the wind freshened and the sun was fast sinking, but they managed to hold on to Green who they got into the other boat and pulled alongside, when she also nearly sank owing to hot weather having opened the seams of both boats. They afterwards recovered the other boat. March was much exhausted. On receiving our patient we rubbed him dry with hot blankets and laid him in his berth putting a stone bottle of boiling water to his feet and a blister to his chest, two emetics were given which however had a contrary effect, animation soon appeared and his pulse beat 60 and five minutes after 110. I remained up with him all night.

8 Mar

Green much better. The Captain has stopped his grog for the remainder of the passage. A subscription of £2.0.0 was raised aft for March.

9 Mar

The subscription fund found its way to us in the morning and I gave 2/- for although I am at a saving age when every penny is an object I shall always be one of the first to reward such gallant conduct as that of risking one's own life to save others.

10 Mar

Martin, one of the sailors was put in irons and charge of him given to Walter by his father, he (Martin) having been detected in purloining a case belonging to Mr. Bateman and selling the contents (linen) to Mrs. McDonald. I cleaned out the medicine chest thoroughly in the morning. We have a light fair wind for the Cape.

11 Mar

Mr. Carter dressed Pritchard's, McDonald and Johnson's ulcers in the morning and I made up some medicine for the latter.

12 Mar

A very stiff breeze and quite fair running, 8, 9, 10 knots.

13 Mar

Peacock fell down the hatchway in a fit to which is subject, Mrs Pollyblank became hysterical at the same time. Mr. C. bled Dillon, who fainted immediately.

14 Mar, Sunday

Prayers as usual A.M. Slept on deck with Walter all night.

15 Mar

Mr. Carter bled Mr. Daley in the morning. Mrs. C. instructed me to knit a fishnet.

16 Mar

Fine breeze, Doctor pulled out a tooth for Sam Duval. I have at length learnt the art or mystery of knitting, alias netting.

17 Mar

A squall the forerunner of a stiff breeze came on at 4 p.m. All hands were called on deck to shorten sail.

18 MAR
Strong breeze, 5 points out of our course; nothing in the aftn.

19 MAR
Stiff contrary wind her head lying S.W. 7 points out of our course, S. lat 290 Long 7½W.

20 MAR
Wind shifted rather more favourable, we wish to run up to Eastward.

21 MAR
The wind has come round within 1 point of our course. Made up medicine for Bateman's children and others.

22 MAR
Favorable wind continues. Long 4½W. Knitting in the afternoon.

23 MAR
Made up medicines for Savory & others in the morning, knitting in the afternoon, wind fair yet.

24 MAR
Mr. C. extracted a tooth for Mr. Schields, Boy Sam and one for Cooper, alias 'Long York', and broke his gum lancet in the operation.

25 MAR
Her head direct East, we are in the Latitude of the Cape. Peak & Watts had a skirmish but were parted by Mr. Sargeant.

26 MAR
Expect to be in the Table Bay in a week. Light, variable winds.

27 MAR
Finnis fell down and hurt his hip seriously. Downes had two teeth extracted. I was sitting on the combings on the hatchway during the first watch, talking to Scantlin who was telling me about the Hindoos, when the boatswain (Anderson) took me up suddenly and dashed me on the deck. On expostulating with him, he attempted to drive me aft and fell upon me in his attempts and afterwards threatened to throw me overboard. The man was quite drunk and, as I knew it was useless to contend with one in that state, I went below to my berth. My friends March and Holbrook (Capt. Ascott's nephew) on hearing the facts went up to Anderson and each offered to fight him and Holbrook got a blow in his face from the boatswain.

28 MAR, Sunday
Prayers as usual in the cabin. Boatswain came to me in the morning and begged my pardon for his rough behaviour last night and wished me to tell him how it took place, as he had not the least recollection of it himself. For my part I was so surprised at being dragged from my seat while in quiet conversation that I hardly knew what happened. However knowing him to be a quiet man when sober I shook hands with him and shall think no more about it.

29 MAR
Charlotte Dyer, Mrs. Carter's servant, and her uncle Curtis the steward are both ill, made up medicine for them.

30 MAR
Wind foul being E.S.E. and the sea running high, the water rushed in the Carters' cabin in the afternoon and set it afloat. Old Atkinson made a dish of 'lob sconce' to perfection for dinner.

31 MAR
Foul wind all day, got out our clothes and aired them in the poop.

1 APR
Wind fair all the morning but shifted to the old quarter at 4 p.m. I made up some medicine for Mr. Atkinson etc.

2 APR
Several immense large black fish were seen from the bows in the morning, the largest appeared in length about 30 feet. Made up a mixture for Fearless p.m.

3 APR
Curtis the cook was seized with dumbness arising from inflamation of the mucous membrane of the throat, on application of a purgative speech was restored.

4 APR
A fine clear day. Mrs Jones on the sick list. The wind fair until 8 oclk p.m. when we had it from the S. East.

5 APR
The sea almost covered with shoals of black fish in all quarters, light variable winds and a strong current setting us off the Cape.

6 APR

About 300 miles from the Cape and too far to the Northward. Cleaned my gun thoroughly.

8 APR

A fine fair breeze, expect to make land in a day or two. Charlotte very ill (*chlorosis*).

9 APR

Breeze fair but scanty, wrote Mr. Benningfield's journey for him in the evening.

10 APR

A fine free trader about our size passed us within three miles homeward bound. We had all our studding sails up, fair wind.

11 APR

A barque was seen coming up astern in the morning, but the wind freshening, we cracked so much sail on the old lady as to lose sight of her altogether.

13 APR

Up at daybreak on the fore top sail yard looking out for land. A bark was seen ahead, and one of the larboard quarter just perceptible. The wind was fair and just of the strength which would admit of all sail. We set two main studding-sails, two fore-topmast do., main and fore-top-gallant ditto, and also royals. The bark ahead did the same and being very light we could not come up to her, she also set a flying jib which we had not. Another large barque came very near but kept astern of us, all bound in the Cape. We got 9 knots out of the old *Medina*. About 9 o'clk land was seen ahead, and every soul on board crowded on deck to see the wished for terra firma. Table Mountain with its flat surface, Lion's Head and Rump next showed themselves distinctly, the latter mountains an exact representation of a Lion sitting down.

Gradually the water changed colour and appeared a green hue as we neared the shore. We soon descried some beautiful detached dwelling houses on a place under the rump which Mr. Stockenstroom (who is a native) says is Green Point and Sea Point. The breakers on the beach were next visible and with a glass we saw a man on horseback coming from Cape Town. [*Cape Town had been established as a provisioning and watering station for Dutch trading ships in the mid-17th century and was occupied by the British during the wars with Revolutionary and Napoleonic France and ceded to Britain in 1814. By 1840, it had an Anglo-Dutch population of 20,000.*] the demand was up at Lion's Rump for our name which we answered. As we approached nearer the shore we saw fresh beautiful objects, the little white houses with shrubbery and gardens before them were extremely lovely.

About 6 o'clk p.m., we were abreast the Lighthouse and at ½ past 6 anchored

30. Table Bay in a Calm; watercolour by Thomas William Bowler, 1857.

in Table Bay off Amsterdam Battery about 4 miles, when the Port boat visited us with the doctor of health etc. Very bad accounts came in this morning from Swan River [*the Swan River settlement in Western Australia*] by a brig called the *Skerne*. At 8 o'clk Table Mountain was covered with a cloud called The Devil's Table Cloth, when it blew very fresh out of the Bay.

21 APR
Sent ashore for Mr. Carter to dress March's finger which was dangerously mutilated between two casks. He came on board, dressed it, and also Smith the sailor who got a severe blow fighting last night, the vein bled freely in the evening when I was called and prevented further haemorrhage by compresses.

22 APR
Dressed Chartres' leg in the morning, and sent my Mother's letter to the Post Office.

23 APR
Writing a letter to my Cousin Lewis, attended to March, Downes and Chartres.

24 APR
In the afternoon the crew came out on the quarter deck to request liberty for to-morrow, which the Captain denied them when the one and all struck work. Captn. Pace immediately went ashore and sent officers off to put them in prison. Previous to going I gave March and Holbrook ½ a sovereign between them to make the prison bearable on a Sunday.

25 APR, Sunday

Mr. C. came on board in the morning, a fine clear day, a large free-trader homeward bound from Bombay the *Rachel* came in harbour and anchored near us in the afternoon.

26 APR

All the crew came on board in the afternoon the dispute having been amicably settled before the Magistrate by the Captain allowing the men liberty to go on shore.

27 APR

On board all day. Mr. C. told me he intends stopping here.

28 APR

As the Captain will not allow Mr. C. to remain here, being surgeon of the vessel, he will leave Mrs. Carter here and go on to the Swan with self and Johnson, returning to the Cape on disposal of his stock of provisions, house, etc. [*So the pregnant Mrs. Carter and her maid were left in Cape Town, while her husband, his apprentice and his manservant continued to the Swan River Settlement in Western Australia.*]

29 APR

The last of the Cape cargo discharged to-day. We are to sail on Sunday.

30 APR

Went ashore with Mr. C. and Johnson in the morning. I met Atkinson and went with him to the Races which are held out at Green Point about 1½ miles from Town. The races were very inferior but there was a good assemblage of Company, we took some ale and other refreshment on the course. I slept with Atkinson at his lodgings.

1 MAY

Purchased a few oranges for sea stock before breakfast, went to the jetty and stayed a long time for the Steward and went on board in the ship's gig.

2 MAY

Wrote a letter for my brother George at St. Helena and one for Munday's servant, Joe Dicks, to his friends at Warminster. The Table Mountain was on fire in the evening owing to some brushwood having caught light at its base and gradually extended in fantastic forms, nearly to the summit; it looked very pretty indeed and seemed like a flowing wreathe of flowers.

3 MAY

Helping Johnson pack a case in the hold all morning. Sent my letter by Atkinson to the Post Office. The fire in Table Mountain became visible after sunset, it is much more diffused to-night, and looks something like irregular rows of illumination lamps in the form of garlands.

4 MAY

Mr. Carter brought two goats and two kids on board to take on with him. The Blue Peter [*a blue and white signal flag indicating that a vessel is shortly to sail*] was hoisted on the head of the fore royal mast.

5 MAY

Messrs. Venn and Stockenstroom came on board in the morning and abused Mr. Carter; the quarrel originates in Savory's affair, having called him a rascal before Mr. Sargeant the Chief Officer. Mr. C. went ashore and commenced an action against them.

6 MAY

Busy all day getting out Mr. C's luggage which Johnson and I took ashore, hire 4 coolies to take the goods up to Mrs. Ruysch.

7 MAY

The crew employed all day in getting our large cases out of the hold which was done with much difficulty as our longboat was hoisted in.

8 MAY

Mr. Carter's last case came out of the hold to-day. Wrote two letters, one for my Mother and another for Lewis to go by the *Porcupine*.

9 MAY

The barque *Henry* from London came in harbour this morning. Mr. Williams whom we had left behind came in her, and was rejoiced to find his wife had not gone as he feared.

11 MAY

Shipped two fresh hands in place of Smith and Martin, who were turned out. The following passengers we leave here – Mrs. Carter and Charlotte, Messrs. Stockenstroom, Venn, Benley, Savory, James, Westcott, Pollyblank, Lever, Murrell, Dillon, Daly, Lamont Perring, Coopers (2), Hardacre, Howell, Adams, Fearless, Benningfield, MacDonald their families and a few others. March and Crap the apprentice have 'slipped cable'.

Chapter Ten

On to Australia

12 MAY, 1830

Got under weigh early in the morning. It blew a gentle S. East breeze, we went out between the main land and Robben Island, the leeward channel. About now the lofty Table Mountain and Lion's Rump seemed but a miniature of these stupendous hills.

13 MAY

Land completely out of sight and a fair breeze. Captn. Pearce [*passenger*] in a fit in the evening owing to excessive drinking.

14 MAY

Becalmed. We caught several Cape pigeons in the afternoon with fishook baited with pork, and dropped astern, this bird's plumage is very beautiful, the flesh is not good.

15 MAY

Caught a large blue shark, a stiff N. West breeze arose, when we spun along swiftly before the wind, ship rocking terribly. Two casks of Constantia fetched weigh in Mr. C's cabin P.M. [*Wine from the Cape, a favourite of Napoleon when on St Helena.*]

16 MAY

Breeze increased to-day, jib, top gallants and try-sails all furled, no sail set on to mizzen, being in a bad state.

17 MAY

Gale continued all day, fortunately in our favor, the sea running very high, the fore, fore topsail, and main top-sail all close reefed together with the stern staysail only set.

18 MAY

The wind increased to a regular storm, the sea running mountains high, a close-reefed foresail and fore top-mast stay sail were the only two sails set and with these she went 9 knots through the water.

19 MAY
Breeze moderate, fair, running along fast towards Swan River.

20 MAY
1250 miles from the Cape at 12 p.m. Breeze still fair.

21 MAY
On the starboard tack, wind having shifted, made up some medicine for Chartres.

22 MAY
Helped Johnson stow Mr. C.'s cabin in the morning, by putting extra cleats, etc., etc., to his cases and casks.

23 MAY
Mr. C. examined me in simple surgery, and gave me a medical book to read.

24 MAY
Wind fair right aft.

25 MAY
Reading below greater part of the day. We feel much more comfortable since the passengers left us at the Cape.

26 MAY
Wind still fair, the Cape Pigeons and other sea-fowl continue to hover about the vessel.

27 MAY
Mr. Bateman's child died in the evening of enteritis; he has been lingering a long time.

28 MAY
The funeral of the child took place in the same manner as Mr. Benningfield's. Gave the sailmaker a lotion for his hip.

29 MAY
The wind took us by surprise at 6 o'clk p.m. when we were going 11½ knots through the water, unprecedented since we left England. The storm staysail (a new one) was rend in ribbons by the wind, and was secured with difficulty. Martin's boat got adrift and broke off her bows. All hands were ordered on deck

during the night for the storm was tremendous and poor 'chips' [*the carpenter*] was expecting a mast would go.

30 MAY
Wind strong and fair, Pritchard came on the list today.

31 MAY
Reading nearly all day, we continue our course. At night it blew very fresh and there was a terrible rumpus amongst some crockery ware and a pewter basin belonging to Mrs Downes.

1 JUN
Reading below and shuffling up to cool fresh breeze on deck at intervals. She is a good old sea boat and although she pitches confoundedly, still (as the song says) –
> I love the strife
>> Of a seamans life
> And I love the dark blue sea.

2 JUN
A large albatross was *hooked* by Mr. Williams. It measured from tip to tip of each wing 7 feet and was killed for stuffing.

3 JUN
Made up a lotion for Mrs. Williams arm. Reading below all afternoon.

4 JUN
As expected in the afternoon we hove in sight of Amsterdam Island [*in the Indian Ocean, about half way between Africa and Australia*]. At 8 o'clk p.m. we were broadside of it, laying on the larboard side. The moon shone beautifully on the white and dark coloured cliffs, there is nothing remarkable in its appearance, it is rather high but evidently sterile.

5 JUN
Continue with a fair wind. Covered some of my books in the afternoon.

6 JUN
With Mr. C. in his cabin all the morning, and reading solus all the aftern.

7 JUN
Going at the rate of 8 knots all day, a strong breeze.

8 JUN

Amused myself with John Munday shooting at the birds, but could not kill one owing to the ship's rolling very heavy.

9 JUN

A few of the carrier pigeons were shot by Munday. Made some *Infus: Senna: Compes: Ph: Laud.*

10 JUN

Breeze fair but slack. We are 650 miles only from our port.

11 JUN

Very little breeze, the yards square, going 3 knots only.

12 JUN

Almost a calm, the sails flapping to and fro, we are 3 days sail from the coast with a fair breeze.

13 JUN

Little wind but a frowning atmosphere which led the sailors to say something was *brewing* aloft. 6 p.m. foul breeze.

14 JUN

Busy bottling off the Doctor's sweet [*Constantia*] wine all day; Johnson and I had a bottle from Mr. C. when finished.

15 JUN

Wind to-day to use a sea term is "all ways and no ways", we were on the larboard tack in the evening.

16 JUN

Wind round to the N.W. set sail accordingly.

17 JUN

The wind moderate and fair until sunset when it dropped and a foul breeze sprang up during the night.

18 JUN

On the look out for land, a very fine day and particularly warm.

19 JUN

Up at 4 a.m. and saw the moon rise at its wane, which amply repaid me for my

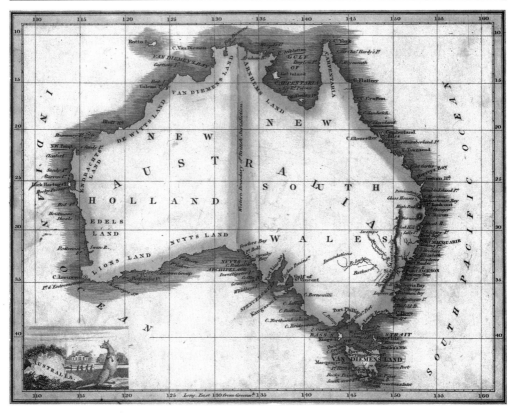

31. Australia as it was known c.1830.

trouble. We hove in sight of Western Australia at ½ past 10 a.m. and continued on to get soundings, although some sixty of seventy miles to leeward of our port. We entered a kind of bay and the weather being beautifully mild and clear, we saw the land to advantage. It seemed very woody and the fine sandy shore on which the sun shone brightly seemed very tempting and I felt a longing sensation to tread on land where perhaps civilised man never walked. At ½ past 4 p.m. we sounded, when to the surprise and consternation of us all there were only 16½ fathoms of water, when we were expecting to be in at least 50 to 60 fathoms deep. The ship was instantly got about. At sunset the wind increased very much when we were bearing off the land as much as possible.

20 JUN
Wind increasing all day, at 4 p.m. it blew violently, when the fore and main sails close reefed were only set, but still strengthening. The fore sail was furled and the fore topmast stay sail hoisted to steady the vessel, at 5 p.m. it was carried away by the hurricane being fairly ripped from the stay. We lay to during the night, with a heavy sea breaking over us occasionally.

21 JUN

The sea very high this morning and our vessel labouring heavy under a close reefed main topsail, the hurricane at its height. 12 p.m. land seen to leeward. 1 p.m. land over the lee bow the vessel drifting towards it without making any headway.

I could see the Captain and Mate were much alarmed although they endeavoured to conceal it while advising together, and the stoutest and most experienced of the men trembled with fear. At this time our main topsail split, but being double remained full, the fore sail close reefed was then set and the helm luffed as much as possible. Still we could not clear the point of land. Towards evening the wind providentially shifted a point or two which enabled us to clear the land, a very stormy night.

22 JUN

The wind decreased a little in the morning, which enabled us to carry more sail. The land, to our joy, is no longer in sight, the sea continued breaking over us all day.

23 JUN

Wind increased to a fearful pitch in the afternoon, obliging us to shorten the small quantity of sail we had set.

24 JUN

Blew a hurricane all day, we were lying to with our main top sail close reefed.

25 JUN

The wind suddenly dropped 2 a.m,. and a fair breeze sprung up by noon, when we saw some whales spouting, but we had a very heavy sea to contend with.

26 JUN

The yards square and all sails set. At noon we were only 56 miles from Swan River.

27 JUN

Fair wind until noon when it changed. This is very vexing for had it continued a few hours longer we might have been in harbour. Owing to the late gales, the fore top sail yard was found to be sprung in the afternoon when it was sent down, and a new one being made.

28 JUN

Fresh breeze all day and foul, steering to the westward.

29 JUN

Foul wind all day, it has driven us sadly off port, being 200 miles from Swan River at 12 p.m. [*The mouth of the Swan River had been chosen as the site of a new British colony in 1827 by Captain James Stirling, R.N., on the instructions of the British Government, which believed that France and the United States planned to establish their own colonies on the west coast of Australia. In 1829, Captain Sir Charles Fremantle, R.N., took possession and a colony was formally declared. The principal settlement was named Perth after the birthplace of Sir George Murray, Secretary of State for the Colonies, and two further towns, Fremantle and Guildford were planned at the same time. In March 1830, some fifty ships carrying about two thousand emigrants arrived but, finding conditions so primitive, many returned to the British Isles or settled in other colonies.*]

30 JUN
Fair N. West breeze in the afternoon when we crowded all sail but it soon increased so as to oblige our taking in nearly all canvas.

1 JUL
Very stormy in the evening, the hatches were battened down as the sea was breaking over us continually. Did not sleep all night owing to her rolling, as we are scudding under a close reefed main topsail.

2 JUL
The storm has done much injury aft: during the night a heavy sea struck the quarter gallery attached to Mr. Carter's cabin and carried it away, the water rushing in and deluging the cabin, when the whole of Mr. Carter's heavy packages, casks, etc., gave way together with chest of drawers etc. etc. and broke through the bulkhead of Mr. Williams' cabin adjoining and made the two apartments into one. Fortunately all the parties were sleeping in cots, or their lives would have been endangered. It was for some time impossible to relieve the inmates as both of the cabin doors were blocked up with the packages and a hole was accordingly made through Bailey's old cabin, when the carpenter and a few stout hands nailed up the cavity of the absent quarter gallery to prevent the further inroads of the sea. The two cabins were in the most deplorable condition and strewed over with fragments of broken furniture. It took us the whole day to adjust them. There was a fine mixture of *wheat* and *shot* over the place.

I could not refrain a laugh when I saw little Mr. Williams with spectacles on nose, peeping through the hole and vowing vengeance on the Doctor for allowing his heavy goods to break his wife's dressing table and all the chamber utensils to atoms.

3 JUL
The storm subsided in the afternoon when we made all sail and continued at a rapid rate. Mr. Nash crushed his finger very badly in the fore hold between two casks of beef.

4 JUL

Continued fair wind all day. In the evening we wanted but 40 miles of our port and stood all night to the Northward as the current gets to the Southward.

5 JUL

Made sail first thing in the morning and hove in sight of land to leeward. On taking observation at 12 o'clk we found ourselves 30 miles to the Northward of our port. The weather proved squally throughout the day and obliged us to keep off the land.

6 JUL

Land in sight all the morning and an island supposed to be Rottnest plainly visible. At ½ past 10 we were abreast of this and laid to until 12 when we made all sail and entered the channel between the island and the Northward coast making for Gages Roads which lay off the Swan river, which is impassable having a dangerous bar at the mouth. As we approached further in we saw no vessel in the roads but were alarmed when no less than five were seen stranded on the beach. This was consolating with a vengeance. About 5 o'clk the harbour master came on board and ordered us to anchor although some miles from the mouth of the river. He advised 50 fathoms of chain, as it was very dangerous to lay in Gages Roads, as soon as possible. There were 3 or 4 vessels, he told us, at Garden Island.

The vessels which had been stranded by the N. West gales were the ship *Marquis of Anglesea*, Capt. Scott from London a total loss on the rocks off Arthur's Head, the bark *Thames* from Sydney, Capt. Andrew, bound to Mauritius but put in leaky, the brig *James* from Liverpool, both wrecks, the schooner *Emily Tayler* and ketch *Ellen* both from and belonging to India, these last were not broken up but expected to be got off. The *Rockingham* and H.M.S. *Sulphur* [*Royal Navy survey sloop of eight guns*] had also been driven ashore but assisted off; the *Cruiser* [*sloop of 18 guns*] man of war was on the station. Scott gives good accounts of the place but provision was very high and very scarce. We could see a few tents and huts with a glass but the country looked very flat and desolate. There are abundance of excellent fish however, off the river which is a great blessing to the inhabitants.

7 JUL

Several of the passengers went ashore in the morning. We caught several fine fish alongside. The ship is now prepared to discharge.

8 JUL

The long boat went ashore in the morning with the Captain, Mr. Carter and others. Chartres brought back a curious kind of tree called "Black Boy", it is composed of fibres full of resin which burn with a pleasant smell, the outside is charred and quite black with the heat of the sun. It is used for fuel.

9 JUL

Caught a few fish in the morning. Mr. C. still ashore. We discharged cargo but slowly, being 5 miles from Fremantle.

10 JUL

The Mundays came back with the long boat, they gave most favourable accounts of the Colony.

11 JUL

The Mate, Steward, Mundays, Johnson and others left in the morning with guns, fishing lines etc. to visit the island of Rottnest. They missed the vessel on their return and we hoisted lights for them, they did not make the vessel until midnight.

They killed 3 strange birds, three serpents, a small alligator and several kangaroo rats, the latter are quadrupeds similar in every respect to a kangaroo save the tail which is like a rat's, they are rather larger than an English hare.

12 JUL

We had one of the Kangaroo rats stewed for dinner, it proved a great treat. Mr. C. came on board in the evening, he has sold nearly all the provisions to great advantage.

13 JUL

Packing up in Mr. Carter's cabin in the morning and amusing myself fishing all the afternoon.

14 JUL

Packed up my clothes, thinking to go ashore, but the wind blowing very fresh from the N. West prevented me.

15 JUL

Breeze very fresh in the roads, preventing my communication with the shore. Capt. Scott is still on board waiting to remove us.

16 JUL

The *Skerne* brig, Capt. Stroyan, came in and anchored off the bar in the morning. She sailed only *one* day after us from the Cape.

We commenced heaving in cable to get under weigh when, as the breeze was strong, all the male passengers assisted at the capstan. The wind increasing the messenger broke, upon heaving again, when they cried "sheave ho" to re-ship the messenger, all the bars were unshipped last raise which was always left to run back with. This operation I always left to him (Nash) and he was doing so when she suddenly surged and jerked the bar from his hand which went round with amazing velocity – and knocked down James Munday and Jenkins. This bar struck the former in the upper third of his right arm and caused a simple fracture in two places. He was in great agony and we had no splints on board. Mr. C. however set his arm very well with the staves of an old butter firkin. The wind extremely heavy we desisted all further attempts to get under weigh.

17 JUL

Blowing a fresh North Westerly and a heavy sea in which we drifted 3 miles inland then let go another anchor which stopped her.

18 JUL

Munday much better to-day. 7 large fish weighing from 10 lbs to 14 lbs each were caught from the poop. Wind continued strong and a heavy hail storm passed in at 11 a.m.

19 JUL

Both anchors brought up in the morning, first the larboard when it was found to have but one fluke, then the starboard which was broken in the same manner denoting our anchorage to have a rocky bottom. While the ship was in stays I caught a fine snapper with Nash's line in the quarter boat. We cast anchor in the evening as the wind was fair for entering Britannia Roads. The boatswain hurt his ankle in a serious manner with a cable stopper.

20 JUL

Up anchor and off at daybreak for Britannia Roads. Our course lay through a reef of rocks exceedingly dangerous to pass in so large a ship. At one time on heaving the lead there was only *quarter less three* water and we drew 16ft. by the stern having 6 inches of water only to spare. We got through the worst part safely and were in deep water again.

About 9 o'clk I was with Mr. C. in his cabin helping him to bandage Mr. Munday's arm when the ship gave an unusual jerk and then another. Mr. C. turned pale and went on deck. Munday exclaimed, "By G – we are ashore!" and so we were. However I managed to pacify him should there be much danger.

It appears her head had passed over a shoal but she hung astern and in putting her about she missed stays and before she could be got on the other tack took the ground. The *Sulphur*, H.M.S., which we could see at Garden Island immediately fired two guns to know if we were in distress when the ensign (Union downward) was hoisted at the peak of the mizzen. A man of war boat with the Captain of the *Sulphur* and hands came alongside. We got out the long boat and a kedge anchor endeavouring to heave her off but the hawser broke and the midshipman was sent to the *Rockingham* to get another. Our ensign was now hoisted on the fore topmast head by order of the officer, and we soon had a large boat from the *Cruiser* with 30 or 40 hands, also one from the *Eliza* one from the *William*, two from *Freeman* and also Captain Pace with 4 hands.

Mr. C. and nearly all the passengers took themselves ashore and I was left in charge of Boatswain and another patient. All our attempts to heave her off proved fruitless and we commenced discharging cargo to lighten her. This cargo was taken to an island close by. I assisted them the whole day, our situation was most perilous for had a North Wester come on nothing could have saved the ship from instant destruction, but surrounded as I was by a set of brave and gallant sailors I felt not the least fear.

James Munday was conveyed to the *Cruiser*.

21 JUL

All the remaining passengers including Johnson went ashore, the latter took away the rest of Mr. C's luggage ashore and his own, but refused to take mine. Egad! if we are to go down, and there seems a fair chance of it, I should at all events like my traps to be saved. Johnson is a fair specimen of Scotch Kindness.

I was the only passenger on board and although no one else seemed to care a fig for me, the Captain and officers treated me very kindly. We were busily engaged heaving the capstan and windlass all day, discharging cargo and throwing ballast overboard, at all of which operations I willingly lent a hand, and the Captain often thanked me for so doing.

22 JUL

The old lady bumps and thumps about most awfully to-day. Our attempts to get her off were renewed with two fold vigour but equal unsuccess. Most of the heavy goods and a great part of the Cape ballast were taken out.

23 JUL

Up early in the morning assisting to heave the capstan. About 9 o'clk it was supposed she moved, when the Captain and the officer of the *Cruiser* clapped their hands and ordered a lively song, when the men, about 60 in number, struck up the favorite sea song, *Off She Goes With a Stick In her Pack Boys*, when off she did go in reality and we stood and anchored in Britannia Roads close by the *Skerne*, which vessel the Captain brought safely in without a pilot.

In the evening, when the Captain had retired I heard him ask John, "Has my friend Pocock turned in yet?" "No, Sir," says John, "Well then, open a bottle of whatever he likes best." Accordingly we regaled ourselves with a bottle of Dunbar's port over a game of cribbage and then went to bed.

24 JUL

Britannia Roads lie 4 or 5 miles from Freemantle to the Southward between that town and Greenman's Point. It is not a safe anchorage for the *James* is lying wrecked on the beach. On sounding the well, morning and evening, it was found she made 4 feet of water in 24 hours. This results from her being so long on the bank, we discharged a good deal of cargo.

25 JUL
Went with Mr. Sargeant and some others to the Island of Ca.... [*illegible: Carnac?*] where we had to load the boats with remaining cargo. After refreshing ourselves, we sallied out in the underwood penguin-hunting. We found several but they were secured with difficulty as they bite extremely hard. We also took many eggs from their nests which proved a great treat. I went all over the island which is very small being only 1½ miles in length, it is inaccessible on one side and perfectly destitute. Being a fine moonlight night we ran about the shore chasing the seals and penguins. After a supper of birds we slept on some sails under a shelving rock.

26 JUL
After loading the long boat and cutter with remaining packages we left the island for Freemantle. As there was little or no wind we were four hours getting across when landed near Arthur's Head. The town of Fremantle or *Flea*mantle has no very prepossessing appearance being a mere assemblage of wooden houses, tents and two or three erections of stone.

I went to Colling's *Hotel* where I found Mr. C. and dined with him. He has hired Miss Benningfield's little tent which we set up near Collings and close by the side of the river. Mr. C., Johnson and self slept therein at night.

27 JUL
The neighbourhood of Fremantle is nothing but white sand. The river seems a fine one. Went to the beach two of three times to see about our cargo.

28 JUL
Went with Johnson in the thicket to cut some Blackboy, the trees are very thick and high. We cook whatever food we can get outside the tent and the wind prevents any want of pepper as it is always nicely sprinkled with fine and coarse sand.

29 JUL
Cast my line in the river but caught no fish in the morning, a very wet cold day. I slept with Henry on the site of his intended house at Freemantle. Went into the wood a.m.

30 JUL
Went on board the *Medina* for some things left behind. We were 4 hours coming

32. On the edge of the unknown: settlers shooting in a creek through the Swan River bush, c.1830.

ashore the wind being against us. Capt. Pearce has taken up lodgings with us in the *Royal Red Cap Bell Tent Hotel!*

31 JUL
Went in the wood for some Black Boy, and after dinner a short distance up the river found the Batemans who live in a fine large double tent in the Camp Ground. Just about here the place is very pretty. I shot a small gay plumaged bird in my route.

1 AUG
Johnson and Captn. Pearce's servant went out shooting all the morning but returned empty handed. I accompanied them over hill and dale to the lagoons near Britannia Roads in the afternoon but we could see nothing like game.

2 AUG
Fine day. The weather is very cold until 9 o'clk when it becomes warm, the heat increasing until 2 or 3 o'clk when the cold stage is resumed. Captn. Pearce has his house nearly set up. Mr. C. has sold his to advantage and it is being erected. These were built by Manning in Holborn.

161

3 AUG

Johnson and Henry borrowed Mr. Atkinson's fishing net and had a good haul of fine fish resembling large perch. Came on to rain and blow in the evening.

4 AUG

The *Medina's* long boat was driven ashore last night and the tent afforded us a poor retreat.

5 AUG

Mr. C. has engaged our passage by the *Skerne* [*a brig of 121 tons*]. Stroyan has left her and Captn. Anderson put in Command. The two Butters own her, the principal merchants here Leake, Henty and Lewis.

6 AUG

A wet stormy day, staid in tent nearly all day.

7 AUG

The cargo came from the *Medina* to-day as all three of her boats are disabled and her hull in such a state as will require her heaving down at Batavia.

8 AUG

Walked up to the Camp Ground in the afternoon. Saw several of our passengers, Nott, Watts, Munday, etc.

9 AUG

Went 'over the hills and far away' with Mr. Collings and Capt. Pearce sporting. We had two greyhounds with us and in our jaunt started four pairs of walloughbys [*wallabies*] but they were too fleet.

The country is very wild and woody, every here and there are seen the remains of the finest trees which have been burnt to the ground by the natives. This is a wise provision of Providence and, but for this mode of clearing the country it would be long ere this it would have become an impassable thicket. We passed some very pretty and wild spots, some hilly and others level or low. After two or three hours roaming during which we spotted only 2 birds, Mr. Collings brought us out at the half-way house, Melville Water. Here one of the most enchanting views burst upon my sight. Melville Water is situate about 4 miles from Fremantle and about as far from Perth on the junction of the Canning with that river. The opposite side of the river has a rocky bank covered with wild straggling trees. The river is here very wide and the land about the ½ way house is covered with grass to the water's edge. The land here seems pretty good.

We came home after refreshing ourselves along the banks of the river. I noticed a very pretty red house surrounded by trees at the angle of the river. This, I was informed, belonged to a Capt. Graham and was considered the neatest place in the Colony.

10 AUG

Mr. Munday came in the aftn. to have his bandages replaced. As Mr. C. was out I did it for him. A wet night with wind etc.

11 AUG

Cold wet day, did not go out. Mr. C. went to Butters up the river and did not return on account of bad weather.

12 AUG

Saw Mr. Williams in the morning. His house is up and is one of the best here. He is sinking a well on the premises.

13 AUG

Mr. C. is rather unwell from the soaking he experienced yesterday coming from Melville Water.

I went on board the *Emily Tayler* to a Mr. Hall who lives on board and with whom Mr. C. is intimate. Meat is very dear being 1/3 per lb. and bread also remarkably so, I bought a piece of soft tack as a treat and paid 1/- for a small 3d English loaf.

14 AUG

Saw old Knott in the afternoon to spin a long yarn to me about Guildford, an intended town to be built on the banks of the Eleanor, a river which joins the Swan about 6 or 8 miles above Perth and he means to settle there.

15 AUG

Mr. Carter dined on board the *Skerne* now lying off the bar. Scheel came ashore in the afternoon and I went with him to Arthur's Head where we saw Atkinson, Green and others.

16 AUG

Took a long walk by the sea in search of shells but could find none worth having. I went as far as the *James*

17 AUG

Went to the *Emily Tayler* and Mr. Dodds for the doctor. Called on Munday, Williamson etc. in the afternoon.

18 AUG

Set off after breakfast along the shore as Woodman's Point is esteemed a good place for shells. I reached and rounded the sandy point in 2½ hours and returned rather disappointed at the few shells I met with.

19 AUG

Took a letter to Mr. Hall in the morning and walked round Arthur's Head in the evening. Foundations for a new prison are just laid, it will be an octagonal building. The *Marquis of Anglesea* is at present in use for prisoners. The vessel remains upright on the rocks, one of which is complete through her timbers.

20 AUG

Capt. Pearce very ill from drinking too freely. I attended to him throughout the day.

21 AUG

Saw Munday on my road to Manning who has contracted to build the new Fremantle jail. Surely, the governor should have blessed the place with a *church* before spending so much money upon a *prison*?

22 AUG

A wet dull day and fresh breeze in. Saw Jenkins and Atkinson at their hovel in the afternoon.

23 AUG

In tent all day. The flag was hoisted at the post office in the afternoon to announce a vessel coming in.

24 AUG

The barque *Edward Lambe* Captn. Whiteman came in and anchored at Garden Island in the afternoon. She touched at the Cape and brings a letter from Mrs. C. who is quite well. It appears the heavy winds we experienced were felt equally in Table Bay as three vessels were stranded.

25 AUG

Saw Martin whom we left behind at the Cape has come in the *Edward Lambe*. He told me Mr. Daly and Miss Lamont were married.

26 AUG

Preparing to leave by the *Skerne*. Saw Walter Pace (Captn's son) in the afternoon and took a walk with him.

27 AUG

Johnson went to Perth for an amount due from Mr. Wm. Sterling to the doctor leaving me as butler, head-cook, etc., etc.

28 AUG

Johnson returned from Perth. He has shot a few parrots and a large hawk on the road.

29 AUG

Mr. Carter and self left Fremantle early in the morning to go to Col. Meyers who resides 12 miles from town and near Clarence of Peel Town. We called on Mr. Whitfield a relation of his and took breakfast with him, after which he accompanied us. We walked along amongst the trees near the beach, but being in pursuit of a bird I missed Messrs. C. and W. and continued alone along the beach. I arrived at the house soon after them when we took dinner.

Col. Meyers was formerly in the Horse Guards, but had five daughters to whom he could not give a portion equal to their rank in society and therefore resolved upon emigrating to the Swan. Having a carriage, harp and rather useless luxuries by him he wished to dispose of them to Mr. C. for sale at the Cape. His house is a comfortable place enough, and his five daughters fine, well-bred and well behaved girls but are kept terribly in subordination. Mr. C. came to no positive purchase. We saw the *Skerne* going over to Garden Island for wood. We left in the afternoon and on again reaching Mr. Whitfield's it became quite dark. He gave us some real Irish whisky and water which helped us on the rest of the journey.

30 AUG

Mr. Scheel with Nash called upon us in the morning, being ashore on liberty, I went with them to Captn. Pearce.

31 AUG

Strong wind with squalls of rain, I remained at home all day. Martin, who was offered £40 for his boat, has been silly enough to exchange it for a log hut worth nothing, and one of the square built things used to cross the bar with and called a *flat*. Query which of the two *flats* are most sensible, the animate or inanimate *flat*?

1 SEP

Stormy day with abundance of rain, of the *pleasures* of which our tent allows us to make.

2 SEP

Went with Mr. Welsh who lives in Upper Thames Street. The weather cleared up in the afternoon, but as this is the Spring season here we may expect more rain yet.

3 SEP

Went alone in the woods after dinner, shot a bird like a large thrush. I then penetrated into the thickest part of the forest, where the grass and underwood were so abundant as almost to prevent my walking. Here I started two parrots one of which I shot and he dropped in the grass. Upon running up to the spot I could not find the bird and 'to make assurance doubly sure' I very foolishly placed my fowling piece against the nearest piece of Black Boy and retreated to the place I had fired from On returning, as I thought, to the place, I could not find my gun although I examined every Black Boy about the place. On finding myself lost I had the precaution to fill the crevice of a fallen tree with shot and this tree could not be 30 paces from the place.

I was much grieved and bewildered, the remaining parrot calling for its mate and mocking my misfortune overhead increased my anxiety. I hunted about in every direction from this tree which I could always find but not the gun.

Night was now fast closing in and I had certainly forgotten the way home. While hesitating in the fresh dilemma I happily remembered the direction in which the sun set from Fremantle and if I followed that direction I must come out on the banks of the river. This I did and after two or three miles walk through the trees came out of the bush on a hill near Capt. Graham's. It was dark when I got to the tent.

4 SEP

Went into the wood and walked about from 9 until 1 o'clk looking for my gun but without success as the place is so intricate that I could not even find the tree which I had distinguished.

5 SEP

Rose early and went with Green searching for my gun. After ranging about some hours I saw two large birds, and having his fowling piece in my hand was about firing at them when a noise from the spot I aimed at arrested my attention. On looking more closely, we perceived two natives standing within 30 paces and jabbering away as if addressing us and approached at the same time.

As they had two long spears in their hands and we knew not their intentions, we just turned to the right about and walked out of the wood. They were well made men, tho' rather small, were perfectly naked and had a very ferocious appearance being almost covered with long hair. Their colour was of a dark copper hue, the spears seemed about four feet in length and in our opinion quite long enough to go through our bodies.

6 SEP

Went to Mundays who have a pretty little house erected, called on Manning for his a/c returning.

7 SEP

Walked with John Munday to the Halfway House. On returning we struck into the wood and he, being an excellent shot, killed a wolloughby and a wild pigeon. So deceptive is the forest that on coming home as we thought, we came out near the wreck of the *James* which was about 5 miles out of the way.

8 SEP

Paid a man 1/- to go in search of my gun with me. We hit upon the very tree I put the shot in, but could not find the gun which I must now give up for lost. I think it must have fallen in from the Black Boy in the long grass, or I should certainly have found it. So much for my unlucky day, *Friday*!

9 SEP

Johnson and self took some of our luggage to Capt. Andersen to go off to the brig. At home rest of the day.

10 SEP

Mr. Lewis is very attentive to Miss Benningfield, the old coquette who tried France, England etc., for thirty-five years in vain for a husband.

11 SEP

Johnston went on board in the morning. He is to assist them cutting wood until we sail. Bought a piece of mutton as a treat for dinner at 1/- pr. lb.

12 SEP

Dressed after dinner and went to the Mundays. James Munday intends going to Perth to-morrow.

   Mr. C. told me I should have 3 or 4 days to myself to visit the country which I shall avail myself of the first opportunity.

13 SEP

Mr. Dutton the auctioneer called in the afternoon. Poor fellow he is blind with one eye and cannot see well with the other, for it is loudly rumoured that there is an *affaire de coeur* between his pretty wife and the gent in whose house they live.

14 SEP

Mr. C. gave up the tent to-day. His goods were removed to Halls and he will live himself with Mr. Welsh until the *Skerne* is ready for sea. I am to stay with Captn. Pearce.

15 SEP

Went to Captn. Pearce who gives his house up to Miss Benningfield and erects the tent upon his grant of land. I helped Henry to bring in the boxes etc., most part of the day.

16 SEP
Went to Mundays in the morning, found they had left for Kempscott, a new town forming on the Canning amongst the first range of the Blue Mountains.

17 SEP
Went with Capt. Pearce to the old serang, or boatswain, of the crew of the *Ellen*. These men have found the herb growing wild here from which curry powder is made with rice etc. and we went for some curry of their own making. Pearce can speak their language imperfectly; he was subsequently Commander of the *Dawson* brig and *Highbury* barque, both in the West India trade, but taking to drink betook himself to Swan River to join the rest of the 'geese'. So much for Lionel Ripley Pearce.

18 SEP
Johnson came ashore in the evening, old Andersen having treated him ill. He will remain with Captn. Pearce until we leave.

19 SEP
West to Mundays who have just returned from Kempscott, their report of the place is most flattering, the land being excellent and well watered. They intend settling there as soon as they can get up their plough etc. in flats [*boats*], the only mode of conveyance.

20 SEP
To Munday early in the morning when we started for Perth. He lent me one of his guns. Near Dudleys I met Mr. C. who was coming down from Perth. We took tiffin here and paid only 2/3d each for bread and cheese etc.

We then got on a boat and were rowed to Perth. Melville Water is the finest sheet of that element I ever saw. In rounding the points of the river our boat grounded 3 or 4 times, when one of the men had to get out and push her off. We arrived at Perth early in the afternoon.

I went with him to that demoniacal Atheist Watts, who did not ask him even to take a seat. I put up with my old friend Atkinson who treated me very kindly.

Perth is by far more pretty than Fremantle and much larger. The houses have a very comfortable and neat appearance. So thick are the trees here, that one can hardly see two or more houses at a time except by the Governor's Residence where they have been cleared away. It lies very low and is almost surrounded by mountains. The *swamps* which bear the dignified title of *lagoons* encircle the ground here, there may be about 40 domiciles of one kind or other in the place.

33. Perth, Western Australia in c.1840.

Atkinson is building a substantial house for himself entirely of native cedar, it has much the appearance of mahogany. I saw several pretty gardens in a flourishing state and well stocked with vegetables. I peeped in at a room called the Reading Room near the jetty and was surprised at the advancement of the place. I slept with Atkinson.

21 SEP
Took a walk before breakfast 2 miles from Perth. Here the river winds suddenly round. I went over enclosed pieces of excellent land resembling our English parks. They are called 'Government Reserves'. To me who am so fond of verdant places and wild natural scenes, this walk proved a great delight. I returned along the banks of the fine river. There is a fine footpath here and a most delightful walk it is, the land being scattered with fine large trees to the very edge of the water. We passed (on my return) the Governor's house where I saw Capt. James Stirling, the Governor. [*Captain (later Admiral) Sir James Stirling, first Governor of Western Australia, 1829-39.*]

There is a detachment of troops here who inhabit huts built of log wood in the form of a gable top, the officers' houses are neatest.

Atkinson pointed out the Hospital, also the Church, an imposing clean little structure with the bell hoisted up in a tree which grows close to the door. Altogether I was much surprised and pleased with Perth which is the emporium of the colony.

22 SEP

Left Perth at ½ past 5 a.m. when I bid Atkinson (who has behaved like a father to me) an affectionate farewell. Mr. Whitfield and a talkative tailor came in the same boat with me. Mr. W. is appointed Government Superintendent at Guildford. The tailor came out in the *Protector*. He told us many 'tit-bits' of scandal about Mrs. Hall and other passengers which I gave little credence to. He is going away in the *Medina*. I landed at Dudley's and coming along the river winged a beautiful seafowl, its plumage was of dazzling whiteness, and its small feet and eyes were of a bright vermillium color. I took it home alive.

23 SEP

Went in the woods with Henry and Johnson picking out all the straight poles we could find to enlarge the house.

24 SEP

Cutting down poles and searching for them nearly the whole day. Made up Capt. Pearce his quinine pills.

25 SEP

With Johnson in the wood. Called on Munday who is about starting for Kempscott. Met Capt. Pace who leaves to-morrow.

26 Sep

Took a solitary ramble over the hills in the afternoon. Met a horse in the forest which fled at my approach, the horse who had run away from his owner is worth £80 here.

27 SEP

The poor old *Medina* left in the morning with a fair wind bound to Batavia. Mr. C. seems to regret he did not go by her as the detention of the *Skerne* is so great. The *Medina* was taken away from the Swan River to be repaired at Batavia after going aground, damaged and suffering from effects of her arrival in a storm. [*Her crew and passengers were the most ill-fated set that ever crossed the sea. The misfortunes of herself and passengers may thus be enumerated.*

On coming out of dock a man (Lloyd) died. On anchoring off the Nore she lost her best bower anchor, lost a child on the passage to the Cape, and had one of her passenger's cranium perforated by a pistol ball.

Made a long passage (91) days to the Cape and left the following unfortunates there:–

The two Coopers (brothers) who were found drowned in a well together and were supposed to have fallen in quarrelling.

Hardacre who tumbled into a well at night and was drowned.

Gilby who died in a fit at the hospital.

Lamont who expired at Algoa Bay, leaving his family almost destitute.

Henry Maxwell McDonald who after committing embezzlements to a large amount, escaped to England in the Africa, committed forgery there, was tried and hanged.

Morell who escaped from home to avoid an affiliation case, commenced trade and failed.

Sams, an accomplished young man who turned policeman, the lowest grade of Society at the Cape.

Savory bred to the law, turned first drunkard, then boatman, and afterwards worked his passage as steward of the Margaret.

Fearless, a young man of good education who had disgraced his friends at home became a stablekeeper and left in the brig Active bound to Sydney, which vessel foundered at sea and every soul perished, and Charlotte Dyer who went to London and was reported to be in the keeping of Booth, alias Leslie, a Performer.

The **Medina** *experienced heavy gales from the Cape to Swan River and overshot her port, lost two anchors in Gages Roads, got ashore for 3 days in a shoal greatly to her detriment and had her longboat wrecked.*

Of the unfortunates she left are Mrs. Nott who died suddenly, John Thundery who went to Sydney and there cut his throat and Green who was transported for theft.

After arrival at Batavia the cuddy boy John fell down the after hatchway and expired the same night having broken his thigh, arm and 3 ribs – the second mate Schiel was found dead in the streets having got drunk on spree *as they call it. The Medina was hove down at Batavia and underwent repairs to a greater amount than her value, she then took in a full cargo of rice for another port and put back to Batavia a few days after she left having sprung a leak, having to discharge cargo. On a closer examination her keel was found to be broken and she was ultimately condemned. –* John Pocock, 1835.]

30 SEP

Johnson and Henry went with the Mundays to Kempscott. The schooner *Thistle* arrived from Bombay with provisions which will fetch an enormous price.

1 OCT

Took a long stroll in the woods with Tomlins. Capt. Pearce lent me his gun and I shot a large snake which T. almost trod upon. We killed many Lowrys [*paraqueet*], a pigeon etc. and were for a long time completely lost in the thickets.

2 OCT

Walked to Preston Point, was away about 1½ hours and shot 13 different birds in that time, which astonished the natives on my return.

5 OCT

Made up a quantity of calomel pills from Dutton's chest for Capt. Pearce who has an attack of his old complaint – 'The liver'.

6 OCT

Mr. Carter called in the morning to prescribe for Capt. Pearce. He intends going on board the brig next Saturday finally.

7 OCT

Pearce had a delirious attack in the evening and ran out with his sword which he rammed through the bakehouse and vowed he would kill anyone who came near him. He was secured with difficulty and I stayed the night watching him.

8 OCT

Pearce delirious all day. Having charge of him I kept close within from morning till night.

9 OCT

Mr. C. called in the morning, Pearce a little better. I packed up my few traps to go on board on Monday.

10 OCT

With Henry and Tomlins for a walk in the afternoon to see the new jail etc.

11 OCT

Went on board the *Skerne* in the morning found she will not sail for a week. I am in very bad health from the long use of unwholesome junk and biscuits and I am sure to get nothing better here.

13 OCT

Caught several guard fish. They are long thin fish with a horny protuberance 2 inches in length and are good eating. I am trying to get a little jar full of pickle.

14 OCT

Went ashore for a few hours, called on Pearce for a silk handkerchief I had left behind but Henry who is at Preston Point has *taken care*! of it for me.

15 OCT

Fishing most part of the day. I fear we shall not sail on Sunday.

16 OCT

An officer of H.M.S. *Sulphur* came to search for deserters. Johnson went ashore.

17 OCT

The Captain came on board in the afternoon when the men signed articles, so that we shall be off soon now.

Chapter Eleven

Back to the Cape

18 OCT, 1830
Mr. Carter came on board finally.

  Threatening weather in the evening and fresh Northerly wind, we let out 30 fathoms of chain.

19 OCT
The Captain and owners came on board at 10 o'clk and by noon we were under weigh with a light fair wind. We went out close to Rottnest Island which was barely visible at sunset.

20 OCT
A fine clear day, wind S.S.E., our course W. by N. Continue at 4 and 5 knots. The brig having been ballasted with wood is dangerously crank and will not bear much canvas.

21 OCT
Indited a letter to Mr. Holmes which I commenced writing. Studying the *Pharmacopieia* in the afternoon. Wind fair, studding sails set. We are terribly annoyed with fleas and ants which cover our bedding.

22 OCT
Finished Mr. Holmes letter and made a rough sketch of the place, which though far from being accurate will give some idea of the Swan River locations. Wind stronger to-day, going 6 or 7 knots towards the Isle of France [*Mauritius*] whither we are bound.

  There are two passengers besides ourselves on board, one Mr. Gardner a clever scholar and a dissipated scamp, and also a young *lady* who has been under the *protection* of several gentlemen at Perth, but is at present under the care of Capt. Andersen. She is a fair piece of frailty and jabbers French amazingly well.

23 OCT
Fair breeze, squally weather. Wrote out extracts from my log for Mrs. Carter's perusal on our return.

24 OCT
Reading most part of the day, fine weather and fair wind.

25 OCT
Wind aft, top sails reefed, top gallant furled at 7 p.m. when a brisk squall overtook us.

26 OCT
In the S.E. trades. Mr. C. gave me a sealed letter for my Uncle to enclose in mine. He observed that "he hoped that he might always give as good an account of me."

27 OCT
E. Long. at M. 9h" 32° – S. Lat. 27" 27° Drew a rough map of Swan River for my Cousin Lewis which I shall enclose in my letter from Mauritius.

28 OCT
Becalmed nearly the whole day. Writing my Uncle's letter.

29 OCT
Light steady breeze all day giving 4 knots. Becalmed at sunset.

30 OCT
Almost becalmed, the brig scarcely moving through the water. Copied a statement of the Thermometer and Barometer at King George's Sound for the year 1827 for Mr. C.

31 OCT
Calm all the morning. In the afternoon a breeze sprung up, had a heavy squall at ½ past 4 and reefed top sails etc.

1 NOV
Fair breeze, cracked on and got 8 knots out of the brig.

2 NOV
Fair fresh wind, and strong squalls at intervals.

3 NOV
Strong breeze and favorable. I find myself very ill of scurvy from salt provision, our biscuit is all damaged and mouldy and everything unwholesome we eat.

4 NOV
Going 8 and 9 knots all day, the brig rolling heavily.

5 NOV

Continued fair winds but squally weather. Expect to get into Mauritius in about a week.

6 NOV

Warm day. Our mate, 'Long Tom' appears a sad bungler at navigation and the skipper drinks deep.

7 NOV

Still fair winds. Amused myself by having Evans repeat his misfortune when wrecked in Bass Straits on the voyage from Sydney with the Ferris family, now at the Cape.

8 NOV

Writing letters to my sisters Emily and Eliza which Evans is to take home for me.

9 NOV

Continue at rapid rate, wrote a letter for William Robinson.

10 NOV

On the look out for Roderiquez Island all day, which we must have passed being 300 E. of Mauritius at noon.

11 NOV

Continued rapidly all day. Hove to during the night fearing to miss the island.

12 NOV

Laying to, standing in, tacking about, blowing up etc., alternately all day. Captain fears we have passed the island and lays all the blame on Long Tom. Long Tom fears we have passed the island and lays all the blame on the Captain, who says he will stand in for Madagascar to-morrow should this prove to be the case, as we could never beat up against the Trades.

My throat and cheeks are swollen with scurvy as nearly to prevent me speaking.

13 NOV

Land hove in sight early in the morning and very high and rugged. Our course lay through two rocky islands, but as we drew 7 feet of water only and Anderson knew the place well, he ventured between the mainland and the nearest island. We were so near the shore that I could see the sugar canes. We weathered the points rapidly and at 2 o'clk the harbour of Port Louis and the populous town were visible. [*Port Louis was the capital of Mauritius, a mountainous island of 805 square miles, ceded to Britain by France in 1814.*]

A pilot now came on board and ordered our ensign half mast as news had just been received of the death of His Majesty George IV and the islanders were in mourning for him. Soon after, the Port boat came alongside. The Doctor of Health was very particular and examined us severally taking down the names of each individual. We brought up close to the bell buoy and as the wind blows out here at all times we must be warped up among the shipping. H.M.S. *Maidstone* on the station, she is the largest vessel I have ever seen.

14 NOV
The harbour is very full of shipping but freight is good being £5 per ton. From what I can see of the town it looks large and well built. This is the island on which Paul and Virginia [*characters in a popular early 19th century novel*] met their untimely end, the place was pointed out to me. The interior of the island is said to be very beautiful. The sugar, its principal produce is brought up to Port Louis from various parts of the coast in sharp built small schooners which sail in the wind's eye and beat up the various channels of the port in style. *Eliza Jane*, a barque for the Cape and London, went out in the afternoon with royals and sky sails set. Mr. C. and the Captain were ashore together all day.

15 NOV
I was looking at the town through the ship's telescope in the afternoon, the glass resting on the bulwark when the last large magnifying-glass slipped off and rolled into the sea. I was not aware of its being loose. This accident put me in great tribulation and I went ashore with the Steward and endeavoured to get another. We called at Twentyman's the watchmaker and some others but without success.

16 NOV
The pilot came with warps etc. and Commandr. Schonsberg lent us the use of 30 hands when the brig was warped up in harbour. Here all the vessels are moored head and stern and very close together. As we were very light and small, being only 121 tons, we came in so close that the flying jib boom almost hung over the quay. Captain Thomas of the *Protector* came on board.

17 NOV
Went ashore for a short time in the morning to the market, etc. I cannot procure a glass at any price so I shall be completely at the mercy of Andersen who will no doubt make me pay dearly for it. I was in too much anxiety to take much notice of the town but the streets seem pretty regular and well built. The Custom House is worthy of note and Government House, which almost faces the harbour is a large fantastical kind of building in the French style.

There are serious disturbances and outrages daily taking place between the Mauritians, originally French, and the English. The *Maidstone* will move close in to prevent anything seriously occurring.

18 NOV

Johnson is to go to the Cape in the *Leda*, he will attend on the passage to Major Douglas an invalid from India. The *Skerne* will probably be three weeks loading here.

19 NOV

Posted letters to my Uncle, Mother and Lewis. Johnson was upset alongside in a narrow canoe and got a good souse over head and heels.

20 NOV

Went ashore to the market with the Steward. The people here jabber a jargon of broken French, as at the Cape, they speak an imperfect Dutch. The meat is very lean and dear, for all the bullocks etc. are brought from Madagascar and the interior of the island is devoted entirely to the production of sugar. Fruit is moderate but vegetables scarce and no fish to be had.

The Captain and Mr. C. came on board at 8 o'clk p.m. and the latter informed me he had taken his passage on board the brig *Cornwallis* [*187 tons*], Capt. Henderson, and mine. Andersen like a mean unprincipled man taking advantage of these circumstances insists upon me paying £5 for the damage done to his glass which elsewhere I could get repaired for a few shillings.

The *Cornwallis* sails at noon to-morrow and we were consequently packing up. I gave Evans the letters for home but could not sleep the whole night, so much was I perplexed at the encroachment of Andersen.

21 NOV

After much harangue and entreaty Andersen agreed to take *thirty shillings* for the loss of the glass, which I gave him and soon after went on board the *Cornwallis* which lay near us. At 12 o'clk the pilot came on board when we got under weigh, the pilot making each person answer to his name.

On coming to the bell buoy the brig *Maria* was in stays waiting for us and we set sail together with a fine S.E. breeze intending to keep company round the Cape. The island has a highly interesting and romantic appearance after leaving some few miles from port.

The *Cornwallis* is laden much too deep in every corner, I had to make up my bed on some bags of sugar aft with scarcely room left to breathe freely. She is a very old brig and leaky but a good sailer. The Captain is owner, he seems a gentlemanly fellow and is very fond of cracking me.

22 NOV

The *Maria* a long way astern at daybreak, altho' she put up much more canvas than ourselves. We therefore shortened sail and spoke to her wishing them farewell. When we reset sail we shot ahead, wind strong and fair, our decks

34. A brig of 1830. A model made in Mauritius and bought at the Cape in 1995 by Lewis Pocock's great-granddaughter, Marjorie Holder.

constantly wet from pumping. The cables were stowed in my place which rendered it the more confined for me.

23 Nov
Fine fair breeze all day. She is a regular old tub and has to be pumped every two hours besides being a bad sea boat. The mate, Toby, ordered the 2nd Mate to stow 13 bags of sugar where I sleep. This was a completion of my misery and I had to crawl on my hands and knees to bed but the place was so intolerably close I could not sleep as there is not 2 feet space from the deck. I have heard of there being 'worse shifts at sea' but methinks this is bad enough.

24 Nov
Wind on the quarter, the main, royal, top and top gallant studding sails set, also the foretop and lower studding sails. Going 8 knots.

25 Nov
Wind shifted slightly, in bracing the yards we kept our course however.

26 Nov
Wind veered to the Southward, changed and went on the larboard tack.

27 NOV

Fair moderate breeze in the morning when we clapped all sails on her. I hope to make a good passage and end my misery.

28 NOV

Steady light wind, right aft, crowded all sail. I am very miserable for want of books to read or other amusement.

29 NOV

The water around us a light green colour as if we were over a bank of sand, but this appearance is owing to fish spawn upon its surface. Foul wind being due South.

30 NOV

Wind changed and she steered her course. Came on to blow heavy at 11 p.m. when the hatches were battened down and I nearly suffocated in consequence.

1 DEC

Flashing through the water with a fine breeze, the decks are constantly wet as she ships heavy seas.

2 DEC

Mr. C. had his large chest up to get it painted. Like myself, he is suffering from scurvy.

3 DEC

Fair wind, moving 8 and 9 knots all day.

4 DEC

150 miles S. of Algoa Bay [*east of Cape Town*] at 8 a.m. Wind still favorable.

5 DEC

Going on the larboard tack at the rate of 4 knots, becalmed in the evening.

6 DEC

Becalmed all day. At 7 p.m. a light breeze. 8 p.m. both watches out reefing sails, glass low and dirty clouds running N. West.

7 DEC

A sail descried at ½ past 10 a.m. on our weather bow - not unlike the *Maria* - is a large brig. At 12 we tacked about which she did also. After this we got considerably the weather beam of her, but lost sight at sunset altogether.

8 Dec

Land seen to leeward near Algoa Bay at 6 p.m. and a sail to windward. Tacked about and sounded at 8 p.m. Got 50 fathoms line down. 11 p.m. fresh foul breeze.

9 Dec

Blowing heavily at 6 a.m. and a heavy sea in. At noon it was a dead calm.

How wonderful a change in the most wonderful of elements, the sea, in so short a space of time!

10 Dec

Land in sight all day, very black and mountainous. Several shoals of fish passed us making for the shore, they made a kind of noise resembling a steam vessel but louder. Foul wind in the afternoon.

11 Dec

Becalmed untl 12 o'clk, when a fair S.E. breeze sprung up. Set all sail accordingly.

12 Dec

Fair breeze in the morning, rigged up every studding sail we could muster, when it changed blowing direct in our teeth, This was very provoking as we are only 3 days sail from Table Bay. At 6 p.m. we tacked about being close inshore. The weather was foggy, but at intervals the sun's beams brightened the white cliffs which were studded with moss and seaweed, having a pretty appearance which effect was heightened by the dark craggy mountains behind and the gloomy aspect of the sea.

13 Dec

Beating up against a fresh North West breeze all day which slackened a little at sunset.

14 Dec

Foul light breeze all day, made land again at 4 bells p.m.

15 Dec

Becalmed all day. Captain and hands whistling for a breeze and singing, "Blow, winds, blow!"

16 Dec

A brig seen on the lee quarter at sunrise which Toby knew to be the *Usk*, a Cape coaster, as he was formerly mate of her. A light fair wind sprung up at noon when we made all sail and the brig dropped astern.

17 DEC

Saw the *Usk* far astern in the morning. We continued with all sail set before the wind at a speedy rate, expect to reach port to-morrow.

18 DEC

Passed true Cape Point early in the morning. Soon after sun, a schooner ahead and a bark and the *Usk* astern all making in for Table Bay. At 9 o'clk we were behind Table Mountain which has quite a different appearance when made from the Northward. The breeze being strong we rigged in all our studding sail booms and the wind slacked when abreast of the Rump. The bark astern had every stitch of canvas wet and looked like the *Leda*. Now Mr. C. had a bet of a new hat and umbrella with Capt. Robb of that vessel that the *Cornwallis* would arrive in harbour first and he was in a terrible stew about it. The schooner kept ahead, she was the prettiest rakish craft I ever saw and proved to be the *Courier*, Capt. Palmer, belonging to Carfax House, new and on her maiden voyage.

We gradually weathered the headlands and about 4 p.m. all four vessels answered the demand from the signal staff. Off the Lighthouse almost touched a small ship working out. We anchored at 4 o'clk and the *Leda* a few minutes afterwards. She has carried away her mizen topmast through cracking on.
I went ashore to tell Mrs. Carter of our arrival, saw her little boy 4 weeks old and returned on board immediately. We have made 27 days passage of it.

19 DEC

On board all day, the mate brought the brig close in to discharge and moored her. The brig *Olive Branch* sailed out for London.

20 DEC

On board all day. Men employed setting up backstays to main mast.

21 DEC

A barque the *Fame*, Capt. Butler, put in with loss of all three topmasts. There is also a ship in harbour the *Greenock* which is hove down having sprung a leak at sea.

22 DEC

Mr. Carter and the Captain took breakfast on board in the morning. I went ashore with him but only stayed a few minutes as I must live on board until he is settled.

23 DEC

On board all day. A large free trader homeward bound came in.

24 DEC

Sent some of Mr. C.'s baggage ashore in the gig. I hope he will soon provide a house, for I am heartily tired of the brig and the sailors' company.

25 DEC, Christmas Day

On board with the sailors. I spent a very different one from the last when at home with family. We had something for dinner which received the cognomen of a plum pudding, the plums averaged between 60 and 70 per acre. Well, I hope they have a better one ashore and I care not if it 'stick in their throats' like this does in mine.

26 DEC

It is very hard I cannot hear from my Mother or one of my friends.

27 DEC

Wonder I hear nothing from Mr. Carter. On board all day.

28 DEC

Two boatloads of sugar taken out of the brig being the commencement of discharging her. Still on board.

29 DEC

Blowing a fresh South-Easter nearly all the day. The steward brought me off some clean linen.

30 DEC

Went ashore in the morning with all my 'goods, chattels, wares, apparel etc.' Stayed at Mrs. Ruysel's.

The Doctor has taken a house in Burg Street

31 DEC

Engaged all day removing goods, drugs, etc., into our new home No. 8 Burg Street, corner of Castle Street. It is a neat little house enough, containing 8 rooms and outhouses. I slept in it solus.

...and then...

In Cape Town, John Pocock remained apprenticed to John Carter but was unhappy. He lodged with his master but Mrs Carter, who was eventually to return to England, proved selfish and unkind. John was expected to stay at his lodgings, was unable to go for the long walks he loved and complained that he could not make friends because the clothes the Carters provided him with were of such poor quality: "For the life of me, I cannot fancy them," he wrote. "That jacket has such a charity boy look about it."

His apprenticeship ended in December 1835 and shortly afterwards Carter's commercial speculations failed and his business went into liquidation. John could not afford to return home to take the examination to qualify as a surgeon, so in May 1836 he became assistant to an apothecary, J.H. Tredgold. A year later he was registered as a chemist and druggist and formed the partnership, Tredgold and Pocock, "with a third part of the profits". When Tredgold left for a visit to England, he left John in charge.

In the same year John fell in love with Lydia Merrington but it was unrequited love and she rejected him in a "cool, collected, almost apathetic manner". He therefore resolved to "put away every carnal obstruction which might prevent the full attainment of heavenly blessings" and became a pillar of the Union Congregational Church, there being no Church of England diocese until 1847. Then, in November 1841, he married Grace Buzzacott from Devon, a teacher at a school sponsored by the London Missionary Society. Their first child, a boy, died in infancy but was followed by a daughter who survived.

He had kept in touch with his family in London. His mother, whose strength of character had held the family together throughout the years or crisis, and three of her children had moved to Chiswick, where the Pococks owned property.

He tried to persuade his brother, Lewis, to join him in Cape Town. Lewis had been working for his cousin Samuel – now a builder and developer as George Pocock had been – but he was not happy and needed little persuading. So in 1842, when he was eighteen, Lewis sailed for the Cape and he too kept a diary of his voyage.

Chapter Twelve

Lewis's Voyage

11 APR 1842, Monday
After a great deal of bustle, packing etc. took a cab with Mother to the Blackwall Railway. A great mind to turn back. Bid Bill Grigson goodbye, went by rail to Blackwall just in time to miss the boat – in great fright for fear of missing the ship [*the brig Galatea*]. Down in the cabin, who should be doing ample justice to some roast beef but the Captain himself, took luggage to Coffee St. & went immediately, & engaged a boat to ship, took cup of coffee with Ma and would not let her come with me. Glad of it afterwards, water very rough, difficulty of getting on board, found my bed not on board, none to sleep on – pleasant, very.

12 APR, Tuesday
Woke very early having slept very little on a bed of sails & ship rocking all night wind very strong in our teeth – lady on board sick already. Pilot thinks he must try to get her under weigh to-day, but afterwards alters his mind. All on board very anxious to get off. Could have got ashore with Captain and another gentleman for 6d head but no price for getting back again named. All the night again lying at Gravesend. Wish I had not hurried so, forgot twenty different things – vexatious, very.

13 APR, Wednesday
The same sight, Gravesend still in view, Church, pier, etc., sick of it. Wish Ma or someone had come down again to see me, thinking how very rough it must be at sea if so uncomfortable here. Pilot weighed anchor at 2 o'ck, beat down the river for 5 or 6 hours and finally ran aground; might have gone much further. Got off again at high water; ship listing very much; lost sight of Gravesend. A great many vessels of all builds in sight, got intimate with Pilot talked to him on deck.

14 Apr, Thursday
Still beat down the river, very much amused. Worked & pulled the ropes like a sailor, far from well tho' not sick. Soon beat down as far as Sheerness began to write a note to Ma – interrupted etc., etc. Pilot expected to go to-day or to-morrow. Weighed anchor after much difficulty, & went on Pilot tonight slept in my berth. Still beating, wind strong against us. Captain read articles [*disciplinary regulations*], etc., etc., in the morning.

35. *Lewis Greville Pocock in Cape Town, aged nineteen, in 1842, by an unknown artist.*

15 APR, Friday
Finished my letter after a fashion, wrote one for mate and one each for apprentices, one Captn. Tayt's son, owner. Boat fetched Pilot. Surprised to see so small a boat live in such a sea, the men look like amphibious animals. Soon lost sight of him & saw the white cliffs of Dover – beautiful sight – two bright lights, seen for miles. Bid adieu to old England, & went down to sleep, sailing briskly.

16 APR, Saturday
Sailing down the Channel, nine knots an hour, fair wind & fine day. Very much amused with the Scotch lingo. The Captain sent the Steward down to tell Mr. 'Pukirk' he would be glad of his assistance on board. Mr. P. got up & went accordingly & helped to pull the ropes. When I came down again had a touch of sickness & had it not been before breakfast should never of had to boast of being seasickness proof.

17 APR, Sunday
A fine morning cold but warmer than usual, Missionary gave us out some tracts to read. Thought very much of home & about your Church time in England; could fancy while looking at water, Emily, Eliza [*sisters*] & all of you preparing for Mr. Noel's. Yes & I could in imagination trace you all there and hear your conversation, too; tho' perhaps when I got you as far as the Chapel in Queen Square I would be woke from my reverie by Stewards announcing dinner.

18 APR, Monday
Beautiful morning. Captain takes a particular fancy to my flute. At his wish the waves of the Bay of Biscay heard *Jim Along Joey, Sich a Gettin' Upstairs* etc., etc. Played the Accordian also wrote some and read some & sewed some; very much obliged to Betsy for the housewife [*sewing materials*], which was laughed at being rather an unusual thing for a gentleman to use. Missionary's lady at needlework same time, gave me black silk to mend inside of coat.

19 APR, Tuesday
Milder day. Captain made me play again – practised the flute with Mr. Archibald, & fond of it, his sister very ill indeed, seasick etc., etc. Showed the old Bible Ma gave me to Missionary, who has all kinds of translations & considers it very great relict – translation being 300 years old....Missionary very nice man.

20 APR, Wednesday
First thing in the morning, a great many porpoises make their appearance.

21 APR, Thursday
Saw a vessel to windward in rig, asked who she was, & she hoisted French

Colours – wind shifted. Ship jumping like mad, much sickness on board. Helped the Mate to do his log at night. Very squally, the vessel continually washed with seas....

22 APR, Friday
Wind shifted to westward beating all the morning.

23 APR, Saturday
Wind still strong & very disagreeable as it was a moral impossibility to shave in the morning managed to do so in the afternoon as the Missionary told us we should very likely cut ourselves if done Sunday. Captain says he'll have no more shaving on Sunday adhered to – on deck most part of day reading, etc. Played with children till completely pestered, all got hold of my name pat, at this moment there is a little urchin bawling down the hatch, "Mishere Pocock"! etc. etc.

24 APR, Sunday
Beautiful morning, read lst. chap of Romans & the book given me by Mrs. Tredgold. In the evening Captain came down and made me start *The Old 100* & after he had gone the missionary & wife joined us in the Evg. hymn. Played the accordion went to sleep thinking of home, etc.

25 APR, Monday
This morning had my first wash in salt water; after breakfast practised flute with Mr. Archibald, saw a large whale to windward & a ship, a barque about 8 mls. off. About this time much teased at night with the continual pumping which is done every watch, soon got used to it, & they might work all night now before they'd wake us.

26 APR, Tuesday
Omission – forgot to mention how continually was annoyed by the noise of weighing or casting anchor, as the cable chain is stowed away immediately behind my berth; so near that I have only to sit up & can see link after link running away, after it has woke me with noise like thunder. In the evening played the accordion & sung with Captain on deck.

27 APR, Wednesday
My excessive melancholy noticed to my no small surprise, by almost all on board – Captain tries to rally me – play flute to him etc, says I never play now & asked me in presence of several for *The Girl I Left Behind Me*. I of course started it but stuck in the middle to the laughter of the company, which made me obliged to get the notes – the news soon got for'ard.

28 APR, Thursday
Miserable wet day wind blowing strong, wrote the log book up for Mate.

Continually 'chaffing' the mates, both Scotch, about their dialect & mimicking them. They began to talk better English as I tell them it is impossible for Englishmen to understand their lingo; nevertheless like the dialect. Steward & self the only Londoners aboard often sit up talking at night or walk on deck getting rather too warm for comfortable sleeping.

29 APR, Friday
This morning shoals of porpoises in sight. The skipper, after a great many throws struck one & we hauled him on deck, & a sailor having cut his head off they took his blubber & liver. Skipper would not let Steward cook any. Opened the Bible & the first ver. I read was Leviticus 11 ch 5 ver. on going first thing below; cut some of the blubber off to make oil, but threw it away afterwards.

30 APR, Saturday
Fluting in morning, etc., & reading in afternoon. Rain major part of the day, went up the rigging to look at a ship. Greased my boots, nearly splitting, with a piece of mutton fat Mr. Vanderscholk (Missionary) gave me.

1 MAY, Sunday
In the trade winds – main boom snapped in two. Comfortable Sunday.

2 MAY, Monday
Saw land to-day, at least most on board did, but alas, poor me, I could only have it pointed out where it was – no spectacles & of course left little telescope at home. One of the Canaries Islands to leeward....

3 MAY, Tuesday
Began to write Ma's letter. Beginning to get excessively warm; put up awning etc. Mr Vanderscholk takes a lesson in music but Mrs. V. wishes to learn accordion etc. Took a lesson *Old 100th, How Bright These*, etc. & one that Betsy sings; first time of missing a music book I think it is the *Scottish Psalm & Hymn* book, like Betsy's, if she will look for it I dare say she will find it.

4 MAY, Wednesday
Got up at 5 o'ck & had a ducking in saltwater, etc., is extremely greasy when soap is used with it but found it much better than I anticipated. Wrote about twenty lines of Ma's letter.

5 MAY, Thursday
Beautiful hot weather now. Played with & amused the children very much to-day till completely 'awearied' as the Scotchmen say. Tried to mend the harmonican, could not.

6 May, Friday

Excessively warm. Unusual noise – discovered a child had fallen down the hatch; I lifted it up, surprised was everyone it was not much hurt. First time of our tasting salt junk [*salted pork*]; Captain won't let us have it again.

7 MAY, Saturday

As usual turned out about 5 o'ck ducked & washed. Captain asked whether I was going ashore having white jacket on, often asked me before the same question; usual when dressed any way out of the common, but it was not a *very* probable thing being about three hundred miles from land which was the coast of Africa. What a watery idea.

8 MAY, Sunday

Service in the afternoon as usual, most admirably by Mr. Vanderscholk, two hymns, etc. – in evening after prayers, ten o'ck, Skipper, Mr. Cormack, and self sung *Old 100th* which was not only admired by Mr. V. but by our worthy selves at the time.

9 MAY, Monday

Very surprised & sorry – no novelties in the shape of rough weather. Captn. says I may keep the novelty to myself. Dull, very. Played in the evening *The Light of Other Days, Donald*, etc., etc., sung with the Skipper.

10 MAY, Tuesday

Had a headache, Scotsman call it a 'sore head', quite a sluggard – not up till 8 o'ck! Often thought of England, etc. Went up to the main-top with the second mate after the dried herrings for tea, wanted me to go up further but wouldn't at that time as I thought Ma would not like it. Herrings very plentiful & quite as nice; wish Eliza was with them, the herrings I mean, she is fond of little messes. Beautiful starlight evening & ladies on deck.

11 MAY, Wednesday

Extremely hot. Had a confab with Miss Mary Archibald on various subjects, serious young lady; mentioned it in Ma's note. Ladies on deck this evening who with us talked & sung etc., etc. Sat with Mate 1st watch.

12 MAY, Thursday

At Miss Mary's request played two or three tunes to her *Bacarole, Angel's Whisper*, etc., which she sung in evening. I wish Eliza had been there, not that I mean to say *she* sings it *bad* but had Miss Mary the words it was most melodious; she is a sweet singer. Tried *Deserted by the Waning Moon* with her. Had the hatch taken off which made it much cooler below.

13 MAY, Friday

Played a small flute. Some time while on the main top with Bill Tate saw a child fall down the hatch, an Archibald, & on enquiry it had "no cut he'sel but brieused his heed a wee bit". Too warm to sleep.

14 MAY, Saturday

A large fish being caught; had some of the monster for tea, very good.

15 MAY, Sunday

Had confab with Miss A. about Dr. Liefchild, Mr. Archer, Dr Redpatch etc., etc. whom she has heard during her stay in town, in Wells St. I mean.

16 MAY, Monday

Captain in a very good humour, variable wind, etc...A squall commenced, & we took all the stunsels in quick, rain in torrents. Subsided to a perfect calm when I went below completely drenched, & jumped into bed.

17 MAY, Tuesday

Rain to-day again in torrents. All had regular wash on board, washed three or four shirts and dipt all my cloth clothes. Capt'n & Mate with self caught upwards of 80 gallons of water. Hung up some of my things on the main top rigging.

18 MAY, Wednesday

Fine morning but more rain, saw two ships ahead. Captn. tells us to get our letters ready. The ship presented a curious spectacle with all the clothes hanging up.

19 MAY, Thursday

Continual calms. Also receive note from sailors to prepare for the shaving match, take ansr. on the end of my sword.

20 MAY, Friday

More rain & very calm. A very bad cold, having been wet too often. Commiseration shown me by ladies, gruel with rum at night, etc., etc.

21 MAY, Saturday

Cold rather better, almost calmed going about ¼ knot an hour. A beautiful fish caught at bowsprit to-day, weighing 21 lbs., call it Albecore [*a large species of tuna*]. Had some for tea, same as last Saturday, beautiful eating. Sailors singing a great deal to-night & nearly every night.

22 MAY, Sunday

Rain in morning, fine afterwards. Service as usual by Mr. V., Scotch tunes sung played on flute, some of Betsy's tunes afterwards....Went to bed at 12 o'ck, very hot & becalmed.

23 MAY, Monday
Got up early & saw the sun rise. Washed of course, had my breakfast, played flute etc., read. Sat on bowsprit a long time, watching shoals of fish playing about, had the harpoon, didn't strike any. Thousands astern and to windward in evening, look very pretty, sparkling like fire, & every now and then jumping above the surface to catch their prey, consist principally of flying fish.

24 MAY, Tuesday
Still calm weather scarcely moving, played flute in morning to Miss A; singing; generally flute is harsh at those times. Most beautiful moonlight evenings, see plainly to read, full moon tonight. Caught another Albecore today. Some of the Sailors very noisy in evening, Geo Lea, principal. Capt. went forward & prevented them fighting, went with him. All quiet again before 12 o'ck,. had been drinking too much in evg.

25 MAY, Wednesday
Crossed the line about 2 p.m. men in afternoon habited themselves in nautical dresses, etc., shave new apprentice & came aft, & first person they approached was myself. Very sorry I was not aware they intended only fun as I struck carpenter thinking they intended taking me forward. I thought it was high time to begin to think of it, when they surround me, & called out "Seize him!". Written, or intended to do so, full particulars in my letter. Passed off very well. Most beautiful moonrise.

26 MAY, Thursday
Early this morning get into the trades, blowing rather fresh. Captn. & self had some sport in morning harpooning Albecores, etc., though ladies must think us great brutes. Mate fainted at time with sore thumb, gave him some water & dressed it for him afterwards, with stuff from medicine chest. Captn. takes a whim in his head to give us salt beef for dinner, accounted for by his fresh provision being found fault with, being indifferently cooked, etc., etc.

27 MAY, Friday
Blowing very fresh, going 7 knots an hour. Thousands of fish to windward, leeward, astern & ahead. Sailors caught eleven in the afternoon, most Albecores; obliged to throw some overboard. Miss A. & Mrs. Vanderscholk sick today. Still sea very high, & decks washed therewith occasionally. As usual, officiated in the place of Captn., he not dining with us for some time except occasionally. Very much pleased with the alteration in the weather from the dull monotony of the calms. Up all the 1st Watch.

28 MAY, Saturday

Wind very high, ship listing much. Just before going down to dinner, the tureen of soup took it into its head to empty itself, without any help, & sundry crockery breaking at time. Some singular amusement this morning (but not in my opinion) on board, as I managed to turn head over heels, with a lurch of ship. Miss A., etc., better, Captn. & I confabing a long while on deck at night till 11 o'ck when there was a bit of a squall, finished his cheese, & took down main top gan'sel.

29 MAY, Sunday

Went on deck at 3 o'ck p.m. during a heavy squall, Captn. on deck; carried away the foretop gan'sel shivered to ribbons. Continued some time, vessel dancing & very much amused therewith. At 9 o'ck wind carried my 'Sou'wester' over the side, & Mate's cap. Heavy seas came over deck often in morning. Service as usual, (Rich Man & Lazarus, etc.) & Mr. Melvill's text 'If they do this in a Green Tree what will they do in a dry?'

30 MAY, Monday

Rough night it has been. Captn. & Mr. V. have some words, & end them by shaking hands, some difference having been between them for some days. Beautiful starlight evening, Ceres & Venus very brilliant, casting a reflection on the waves; ladies singing on deck, etc.; self with them various confabs on various subjects, they used to hear Mr. Vaughan preach at Kensington.

31 MAY, Tuesday

Wind more moderate. Put up the top gallant sails again; caught several flying fish which jumped on board; Miss A. put a very pretty one in spirits to preserve for sending home. While sitting down reading, a rude wave disturbs me, splashing book & self; ship making much water, pumped every hour.

1 JUN, Wednesday

Calmer still. Took the reef out of the topsails, etc. In morning cut Mr. Vanderscholk's hair; wife & himself say 'twas never cut so well. Hopekirk's fault, went to sleep in afternoon consequently sat up late writing, etc., while Captn, Mr. Cormack & self were supping below, a shelf broke down, alarmed us & upset some salt; my ink-stand was capsized last night, contents thrown into the candle box.

2 JUN, Thursday

A vessel this morning to windward, about ten miles off, bore down upon us & spoke, a French schooner. Captain & Mr. V. spoke to them as they did not understand English, & came close alongside, out 70 days from Marseilles. Went up to the maintop & slipped on the rigging after which tore my foot with a nail getting some cheese in an out of the way place.

3 JUN, Friday

Fine day. Getting much cooler; sailor washed some of my clothes, up before daybreak; saw sunrise, etc. Was weighed in the morning with others by steelyard; exactly same weight as Mr. Hannah being 10 st. 5 lbs. Ladies also weighed etc. & children, one child weighed as much as 300 ozs. What a weighty idea! -Shakespear.

4 JUN, Saturday

A ship over the weather bow, with all sail set, going S.W. Could not come up with her. Kept in sight major part of the day, etc. Heavy squalls at times to-day but of short duration. Clean clothes brot 'home' in evening; wrote an a/c out for the Skipper. Saw in evening a monster of the deep, Captn. thought it was a whale.

5 JUN, Sunday

Very squally. Got the earache, headache & sore throat; ladies, etc., said they never saw me look so truly miserable. What a wretched idea!

6 JUN, Monday

Heavy sea. Made myself a dressing case out of the harmonican. Ship rolling a great deal. When I went on deck saw the fore topsail almost carried away; several heavy seas wash over deck. Staid with the Captain & Mr. V. till 12 o'ck, when the wind had partly subsided.

7 JUN, Tuesday

Wind more moderate, hoping it will change more to the westward soon; at present going S.E. Thinking much of England, home, John & Cape. Sea came over the side & drenched several of us, copied some sacred music in morning till dinner time, played the flute with Mr. Archibald some time below.

8 JUN, Wednesday

Vessel & wind quiet or nearly quiet, we managed to shave this morning, after which climbed up in the maintop, & read, edified therewith, etc. Obliged after dinner to remove my bed etc. as the cable chains were both taken out on deck for examination. Have said before that the chain locker was immediately behind my berth. Very calm in evening.

9 JUN, Thursday

Still calm. A ship about 12 miles off to windward going same way & supposed it was same that we signalized a month ago, bound for Port Jackson. Went up as far as the topsail yard with Captain & looked at her thro' telescopes. Getting much cooler.

10 JUN, Friday
Breeze still fresher, going 7 knots an hour, & direct East. All on board talking of & pleased with the idea of being soon at the Cape.

16 JUN, Saturday
At 2 o'ck this morning, woke by all hands being called on deck. Could not sleep, so turned out, & pulled with Sailors & Captain till gale was over, blew very hard, reefed the fore topsail, trysail, & stowed both top gallant sails; up again at 6, wind more moderate, deck continually drenched a great many times. Caught cold, etc., etc. Winter now.

12 JUN, Sabbath
Fine morning but rather cool. Captain in a *very* good humour, could not exactly account for it till I remembered it was his Wedding day, drank his health & Lady's at dinner etc. Divine service in afternoon as usual by Mr. V.

13 JUN, Friday
Very calm in morning, not going more than 2 knots an hour. A great quantity of Cape Pigeons followed us the whole of yesterday, & this morning some forty or fifty, & two or three large birds called Albercross [*sic*], stop down to, & sat on the water for their prey, threw the poor wand'rers some biscuit, etc., which they fought about. Read as usual in evening.

14 JUN, Tuesday
An accident today. Carpenter cut two of his fingers almost off with his axe, very much alarmed him. Mr. A. came forward & dressed it, sewing it up with plaster, etc., etc., with Captain. Completely disabled from doing work, consequently kept his watch to-night. Fine moonlight night till 10 o'ck. Played flute, etc., in evening. Breeze freshens at 11 o'ck pm. while at the pump; obliged to look out, etc.

15 JUN, Wednesday
Breeze still freshens, sea getting very rough. Took in the main & fore top gallant sails, & reefed the main top-sail. A white bird hovering round us, very large. A squally day, some seas came over deck, increased to a gale in evening. Double reefed the main top sail & stowed in fore top sail read & turned in soon.

16 JUN, Thursday
Wind blowing a complete gale, running before it with only two sails set, double reefed. Sea actually mountains high; very much amused with it, just what I wished to see. A White Squall came on in the morning blowing terrifically; went up aloft with sailors during it & helped stow the foretop sail. Long previous to this, I have obtained on board the name of the 'stormy petril'. Of course, wet through to the skin all over. Pumped myself warm, etc.

17 Jun, Friday

Wind abated last night at 12 but, worse, left a heavy swell behind it, ship rolling tremendously. Oldest sailor on board (the Second Mate) never experienced such a night. Drawers nearly capsized, lashed them; boxes wanted to break my leg apparently, pulled the table down, tore my arm with a nail doing so, no table to breakfast on. Seas rolling over the deck all ways, wet everything & every one above, below, up, down, underneath, thro' and all the other prepositions.

18 Jun, Saturday

Wind fresh again, sea higher than before. Going along 7 knots an hour with only two sails set, foresail, & main top'sel, sea came over the quarter, & half-drowned me, happened to have my mouth open, too, of all times. Heavy squalls at times every hour, attended with smart showers of rain. Saw a great many porpoises to-day coming from the N.W. Caught three birds to-day with fishing tackle, all alive; killed for dinner to-morrow. Afterwards miserable below, quite wet, etc.

19 Jun, Sunday

Wet day, wind calmer, 5 knots. All talking of being on board only one Sabbath more. A great deal too wet & miserable to have a service on deck, consequently prayers in cabin by old Mr. H. & with us by Mr. V., read & explained for an hour & half the 1st Chap. of Revelations very admirably. Captain, Mr. Cormack, first Mate & self to listen, sung a hymn after prayers, & then turned in for the night, very wet at times, rain came down the hatch.

20 Jun, Monday

Calm weather, going 7 knots. Set the studding sails above & below, all in a bustle this morning, all busy. Captain & self cleaned our knives & forks after breakfast. Had a piece of rolley poley pudding given me, sweet, very.

21 Jun, Tuesday

To-day you have the shortest night in town, & here we have it midwinter, & very wet. A tremendous storm last night between 12 & 1 o'ck. Woke by the Captain's calling "All hands on deck!" Sea running mountains high, lasted for an hour; much rolling afterwards. Beautiful moonlight evening but extremely cold. Going about 5 knots only, deck leaked very much last night, dripping down on my [*chest of*] drawers, some got inside, put my Mac over them, leaking behind me, too, foot of the mainmast.

22 Jun, Wednesday

This morning put some of my things to right; wrote an a/c out for the skipper; practiced the flute with Mr. A. Wind abated, quite calm evening & full moon. Breeze freshens 10 o'ck. Helped put up the studding sails previous to going to bed & read Acts 1, 2 & 3 Chaps.

23 JUN, Thursday

Thr'out day 8 knots all sail set to the best advantage. Overhauled my 'cloes', etc., in morning. Several seas over the quarter deck to-day; helped haul the flying jib in, etc. Getting rather squally. Invited & went down in to the cabin & had some mulled wine, etc., etc. Staid on deck the first watch till 12 o'ck read as usual & turned in. A very wet night, looks quite wintry, long to be by the side of a comfortable fire, etc.

24 JUN, Friday

Breeze fresher this morning. Set all sails to best advantage; going rather fast, but very wet & cold, uncomfortable both on deck & below. Staid on deck principal part of the night, squall at 12 o'ck. Captain turned out to give orders & slipt down on deck; also First & Second Mate same evening. Very little news to put in this book now, must excuse it, etc. Finished making self a water-proof cap; very comfortable keeps out the rain, etc.

25 JUN, Saturday

Still wet & going 4 knots. Rather tired of doing nothing, being so very wet & uncomfortable. Went to bed in the afternoon & slept until tea time, thinking of John & the Cape. Went in Mr. and Mrs. V.'s berth in evening & had singing, chapters in Bible, etc. Went on deck; staid there with Captain some time, could not see your hand before you, so dark, & pouring with rain.

26 JUN, Sabbath

Raining still. Going a great deal to leeward last night & fortunately took the sun this morning 400 miles from the Cape, very rainy & cloudy. Service by Mr. V. as usual, farewell Sermon not expecting to meet altogether next Sabbath. Two dogs had a battle about 12 o'ck, to the discomposure of the various ladies & gentlemen asleep.

27 JUN, Monday

Wind blowing the wrong way going too much to leeward. Took in the main & foretop gallant'sels & a reef in the fore tops'el. Packed, or thought about it, some of my traps, etc., etc. A ship in sight over the weather bow, bound apparently homeward. Unreefed the top sails in the evening & set the try'sel, etc.

28 JUN, Tuesday

Wind more moderate, set the trysail & royal, etc. again. Mr. Archibald shot a Mollyhawk & we put the ship about to catch him. Hauled the monster up, bill about 4 inches long; measured ten feet from tip of one wing to the other skinned to preserve etc.

29 JUN, Wednesday

Breeze freshened, 7 knt an hour, expect to see land to-morrow or the next day. Hauled up the cable chains in the afternoon, Captain had his chart down in the saloon in the evening, & found that we were forty miles almost S.W. of the Cape. he kept watch on deck all night. Cold, wet, dark, blowing hard, & miserable bed quite a comfort.

30 JUN, Thursday

Up early in hopes of seeing land. Went up aloft to unreef the foretop gallant'sel, & upon coming down the sailor who was with me, bawls out "Land Ahead!" & we were all soon enabled to see very plainly. Went up aloft on the topmast, and staid sometime; made a pretty 'mull' [*muddle*] of it, being mountains considerably to the north of Table Bay. Obliged to turn right round again, all very much dispirited about it, were within 12 miles; got in a bad wind.

1 JUL, Friday

Sailing direct Sou. West all morning. Wind shifted in the evening, while keeping the Mate's watch from 12 to 4 o'ck wind favourable and by 10 o'ck. in the morning we were again going S.E. direct to the Cape. At 5 o'ck saw Table Mountain right ahead &, of course, descried it plainer & plainer till the evening. But when the moon rose at 1 o'ck it was very distinct & at 5 o'ck we were before Cape Town.

*In Cape Town, John Pocock wrote in his diary on **2 July 1842**:*
In the morning I heard that the Galatea from England had anchored in the night. I went up therefore to the port and saw the Governor's orderly with a Report of Arrivals in his hand, which I looked over and found the name Pocock amongst the passengers, which I at once concluded was my brother. Then proceeded to the wharf. On turning into Bree Street, met a party of gentlemen who had evidently just landed. I accosted one and found that he had come from the Galatea. I asked if Mr. Pocock was landed. He said yes and called that gentleman, who came forth. Doubting if it were Lewis I asked him the question and found it was my own dear brother Lew. I was much surprised at his height and manly appearance. He did not know me.

Lewis wrote in his diary:
2 JUL, Saturday

All in high spirits of course, boats in numbers alongside. After breakfast, Captain some male passengers & self took a boat &, walking up the St. leading from the Whf, a gentleman enquired of the Captain for a Mr. L. Pocock, & the Captn. accordingly referred him to me & giving him to understand that I was the party in question; accompanied him home where was introduced to Mrs. Pocock & others; went on board with him afterwards & brot luggage etc. Written full particulars to Ma.

3 Jul, Sunday
Went to church to Union Chapel in the morning and the 'Scotch Kirk' in the evening. Church lighted with gas as an extraordinary circumstance.

4 Jul, Monday
John introduced me to several parties & saw some principal parts of the town....John's old solitary rambles shown us, admire his taste etc., saw the Governor's residence, Military School, etc. etc. pleasantly situated in a grove, called the Government Gardens.

5 Jul, Tuesday
Went with Mrs. Pocock and ladies to Sunday School in evening & met there Mr. Vanderscholk who preached a sermon to them in Dutch. Children very forward particularly the coloured younger children, sing very prettily & have comparatively a full knowledge of the Gospel.

6 Jul, Wednesday
Went with John & Mrs. Pocock to Herschell [*Sir John Herschel, the astronomer, lived at Cape Town, 1834-8*] with others, never spent a happier day. About thirty persons the party consisted of, beautiful garden etc., etc. took a walk in afternoon & saw Herschell's Monument, less said about the beauty the better, quite a romantic place close by to which we went, one stream running above another by means of a trough, much pleased with the beautiful scenery, wild flowers, orange trees, etc., etc., prayers, reading & singing & returned home.

8 Jul. Friday
Latin in the morning etc., etc., went out for a walk with John part of the way up the mountain very much amused with all I saw, particularly with the very extensive & beautiful town & bay & shipping, could recognise plainly the *Galatea*.

The Great Storm of 1842

9 Jul, Saturday and following days
As John intends me to commence my trial in the shop on Monday, the Voyage being *decidedly* over. But the first night it blew like anything, our devoted *Galatea* run with two other vessels on the beach & my brother & self went down in the morning to look at them (Vessels *Anon* & *Speedy*), since which time there has been about twelve more ashore some complete wrecks, one with a most dreadful sacrifice of human life.

I have seen all these so my own eyes can bear me witness. I shall begin with the *Waterloo*, bound from London to New Zealand with convicts, and was a very old vessel... John called me to the top of the house to look at her, and here was a sight

36. A storm off the Cape of Good Hope – the ordeal experienced by both brothers when near their journeys' end. A lithograph of c.1840.

indeed, with the telescope we could plainly discern what remained of her, and I can resemble it to nothing better than a stick covered apparently with so many flies, now they go down in the water, now rise again, clinging tightly hold of the splintered wreck, and every time she rises, or one end of her rather rocks back again above water, we could notice a visible decrease in their numbers. On the beach to make it more melancholy were thousands of people close to the wreck, and their fellow creatures perishing before their eyes....

I went down immediately to the beach (about half an hour's walk) and when I arrived there were a solitary one or two merely still either lashed or clinging to the only fragments that remained, and a boat was then putting off to try and rescue them, but it merely, after some trouble, brought one ashore, who it was very plain had nothing more to do with this world; the vessel at this time strewed the shore for half a mile along the beach, being completely in pieces.

Now for this most singular account of the behaviour of the 'Authorities' of Cape Town. It is not the intention of a simple fellow like me to accuse or excuse, but I will simply relate facts which I have seen & heard for which I can vouch for being true. It appears this ship went ashore in the night, when it certainly blew rather stiff, and at ten o'ck in presence of many persons began to go to pieces or began to assume certainly a most alarming appearance. I merely relate facts. I say just about 10 o'ck she struck a rock, *and in three hours afterwards in presence of hundreds of people upwards of one hundred and eighty persons perished within a stone's throw of hundreds of their fellow men*. They certainly looked like human beings to men on shore – these poor wretches found watery a grave. Will it be believed in England? Can they think it possible? I assure you there is no exaggeration, during this three hours there was *one poor solitary boat*, which had communication between the shore & ship, *one boat!!* and that a *small one* – pay attention – in a large *foreign port*. In Table Bay, some twenty ships riding at anchor, boats of all kinds & decriptions as a matter of course in all directions & here is a vessel going fast in pieces, here are souls perishing in dozens, close to them are apparently all necessary apparatus for aquatic traffic, plenty of boats etc. to convey *goods* etc. from various ships to the shore, close to them are, as I before said, hundreds gazing idle spectators of the scene, calling themselves human, calling themselves members of respectable society; no doubt considering themselves far above exerting themselves in the least to save a poor miserable man from perishing; it was a remark worthy of record which the editors of one of the papers here made 'that everybody, as it was washed ashore, seemed to have made a curse with its last breath'. I could imagine one of their thoughts when about to resign; "See on the beach there! those are what they called men, those are what are called fellow creatures, those are the people who profess to regard all mankind as their Brothers & Sisters, those are the persons who inhabit this town well acquainted with all employment in such catastrophes, & here they can hear our cries and see us perish! for what, for using a little poor exertion, but we are *convicts* therefore must fly uncared for...!"

Day after day some mangled corpse is washed up from the water as fresh evidence, or rather as a remembrance of this Sabbath Day. Yes, here we are about I think twenty thousand in number allowing one hundred & eighty souls to perish under our very eyes; how can we ever make any atonement for this, how can we ever reconcile it to our consciences. What will England say to us?

[*The Cape Town authorities maintained that the sea was too rough for attempted rescue by boats.*]

Later in July:
Cape Town is a very singular Town & altho' it is generally described as being very regularly built I very much differ with respect to this. Certainly the streets are straight & parallel – the boast of the inhabitants – but that is all that can be said of its regularity. I think we may subscribe it to the simplicity of the original builders here, who probably, had not many other ideas regarding it but straight lines, & could not have managed to make the town pretty without these stiff right angles; some of us here are continually exclaiming against the irregularity of London some of us never saw, but those who, after a series of years, managed to take a voyage always found they say everything that is puzzling & perplexing in the streets; but of course we cannot expect much more; it would seem rather curious if we should hear of London chimney sweeps making an eloquent speech in the House of Lords; they seem here to have a universal dread of London, regarding it as the Seat of Iniquity.

37. Cape Town in 1834. The Heerengracht – renamed Adderley Street – with the Dutch Reformed Church and, next to the entrance to the Botanical Gardens, the Supreme Court, seen in a watercolour by Thomas Bowler (1812-1869).

When I first arrived in the town I was struck by observing a waggon being drawn along the street by 16 or 18 horned oxen, a Hottentot going before to lead them & a man in front with a whip thirty feet long occasionally giving them a passing warning that he was there; of a morning these most singular of all vehicles crowd the town, coming in from the country laden with different produces, & this long whip smacking, & bulls bellowing with the hollowing & shouting, make us a noise if not equal in melody, as loud as Julien's *Concerts d'Eté*. The Boers who are the owners of these 'cow coaches' are pretty hospitable when at home for the most part, but on the whole they are a most uncivilised set, being very ignorant, & unconscious that they can in the least be improved. Since I have been at this place, they have been playing all kinds of nonsense till the British Power has told them who & what they are; as an instance of their opinion of the mighty British Nation, one of them in one of their Councils of War, intending going – I suppose with negotiations – in a bullock waggon, saying it was only (that is, England) a month's journey in this way. The War [*fighting between settlers and Africans inland from the Cape*] is pretty well over now what there has been of it, of course it made a very great stir in the town here, particularly among apprentice boys & junior clerks, we want something to put life into the place for generally you would imagine that 'They eat, they drink, they sleep, what then? They eat, & drink, & sleep again'. In town we have a great many bent on nothing but getting money.

201

...and finally...

On his arrival at Cape Town in 1842, Lewis was apprenticed to his brother John, who, when his partner, Tredgold, died that same year, took over the company, which became J.T. Pocock & Co.; it prospered.

In 1847, the year Lewis became established in his profession, he married the twenty-five-year-old Ann Agard, who had recently arrived from England and had become a governess to a clergyman's family. As this family grew, the family they remembered in London diminished. When, in 1832, their kindly uncle, John Pocock, died of cholera, two of his sons, Samuel and Lewis (the cousin to whom John had been most attached), continued to trade through the wharves above Blackfriars Bridge. After a few years they gave this up; Samuel became a building developer and Lewis, a patron of the arts and a founder of the Art Union, which popularised the appreciation of the arts. This Lewis kept in touch with the brothers in Cape Town, sometimes acting as their agent in London.

In 1854, their mother, Hannah Pocock, also died of cholera. Her daughter Betsy had died three years before and the three surviving daughters, Emily, Eliza and Maria, faced hard times. John sent them money but wrote urging them to become governesses. Four years later, Eliza travelled to Cape Town for what seems to have been a marriage arranged by her brother with Daniel Hull of Durban.

Then John himself became homesick for London and wrote that he longed for "the green hills of Hampstead within the range of dear old Kilburn....sleeping or waking, I often find myself trotting up Haverstock Hill." Then, in 1868, his wife died. Imprudent speculation in copper-mining, led to financial difficulties and his only child, Grace, married a John Paterson and moved to live in the Eastern Province. His health was also failing and he planned a final visit to England. However, in 1873, shortly before sailing, he became engaged to Parthenia Martin, the daughter of settlers, who had been named after the ship in which they had sailed to Cape Town.

Leaving 'Thenie' in Cape Town, John travelled to England but it was not the happy homecoming he expected. He arrived exhausted, ill and in need of care and convalescence. Yet his sister, Emily, took the extraordinary step of having him committed to a "lunatics' Asylum" in Peckham, where, despite his protests, he was held for four months. He was rescued by the arrival of Parthenia, who released him and they were married on 6 June 1874 in the Congregational church at Surbiton Park, a suburb south of London; he was nearly sixty and she, thirty-nine. They spent their honeymoon at Cricklewood, "a small village on the Edgeware Road, not far from Hampstead, Highgate and Kilburn".

John wrote to his cousin Lewis, now a celebrated connoisseur, who had been involved in the Great Exhibition of 1851 and was interesting himself in the new

38. Lewis Greville Pocock outside his pharmacy in 1887.

science of photography. "Living for a few weeks in the neighbourhood of Kilburn lately has revived old feelings and memories, which I had fancied were extinct," he told him. "It was impossible to gaze upon the Priory House, in which my father died, and then upon the other house in which your father breathed his last without thinking of past kindnesses received at the hand of the dead and of no few favours bestowed by the one to whom I am now writing...." They arranged to meet again but John's health deteriorated and they never did.

John and Parthenia returned to the Cape early the following year. There he died on 14 February 1876. She wrote soon afterwards when hearing that she had been pitied for her months of nursing an invalid husband, that the acquaintance concerned had been "labouring under a mistake when he, or she, spoke of a 'sacrifice'. I considered it an honour and a privilege to be able to soothe the sufferings and minister to the needs of one so noble and yet so tried as my late husband." Parthenia lived until 1908.

Lewis Pocock and his family settled at George, near Cape Town, where he ran his own pharmacy and his wife, Ann, started a small school. He too had financial troubles in which his brother John came to his aid, and Ann added a boys' class to the school so that he could become a teacher and take charge of it. Their eldest son, Lewis, became a lawyer, while another, William, had become a chemist and been taken into parternship by his uncle at George. All five of their sons and all two daughters married and when Lewis died in 1888 – and his wife a year later – the boy from Kilburn had founded a South African dynasty.

39. Parthenia, the widow of John Pocock (right), shelling peas for Sunday lunch with Lizzie, the wife of Lewis's son William, and her children Bessie and Johnnie, c.1880.

Health and Medicine in Cape Town

The twenty thousand inhabitants of Cape Town lived in some squalor at the beginning of the nineteenth century. The Dutch had inclined to build along the banks of canals, which tended to stagnate and fill with rubbish. The British liked to build facing the sea but the beaches, too, were often littered and sometimes strewn with effluvia of butchers' slaughtering, fishermen's gutting and sewage. Reliance was therefore placed in a wind known as 'the Cape Doctor' to blow the rubbish out into the bay. Apart from illness due to lack of hygiene, prevalent ailments included rheumatism, *delirium tremens* and venereal disease.

There had long been primitive medical services for seamen at Cape Town but by the early 1830s two hospitals had been built and there were seven surgeons, four apothecaries, four chemists and druggists and a surgical instrument-maker. In 1827, the South African Medical Society had been founded as a professional forum. John Pocock soon became involved and in April, 1831, wrote in his diary, "The monthly meeting of the S.A. Medical Society was held at our house, when all the fraternity attended and a splendid supper was provided."

John was licensed to practise as a surgeon and apothecary, sometimes accompanying a doctor on calls, making up medicines, dressing injuries and recording treatment and sometimes making professional visits alone. He gave an example: "February, 15th., 1831: Mr. Carter sent me in the morning to bleed Miss Holland who was suffering from plethora. I resolved to go through the operation manfully, and on arrival at the house in Plein Street affected a perfect nonchalance although my inward feelings were not in unison with my outward face.

"It appears that this was the first time Miss Holland had been bled and it was the first time I had performed the operation but I did not choose to let them know this; her father and mother were in the room at the time and I engaged the old man in conversation during which I carelessly mentioned my errand. As I had approached the house I found my courage 'go out of my finger ends' when and where it was most wanted but I found my spirits return on speaking to Mr. Holland from the circumstances of his being very deaf, for after every sentence, which I had to bawl out loudly, I found myself more and more valorous. On mention of my business I did not look up or down, or, as Tristram Shandy's uncle looked, 'horizontally', no, I gazed triangually, first at the girl, then at her father and then at her mother and was much delighted to perceive in their countenance no surprise or mistrust.... Preliminaries arranged, I punctured the median cephalic vein of the right arm and took 9 oz. of blood. The doctor on my return seemed pleased at my success and I registed this *Venu secto'* in the day book with no little pride and delight."

Note on the Pocock Family

John and Lewis Pocock were born into a London family, which had arrived from Berkshire nearly a century before. The Pococks had lived in the villages around Newbury, where they had been clergymen, lawyers, merchants, maltsters and farmers. One branch bred three celebrated orientalist scholars and travellers in the Middle East (Richard and two named Edward), the marine painter Nicholas Pocock and his sons (including Isaac and William, both artists and, respectively, playwright and naval officer) and Vice-Admiral Sir George Pocock, the captor of Havana in the Seven Years War.

In John's branch, the brother of his great-great-grandfather was one of the backers of the Kennet and Avon Canal. His great-grandfather, Charles Pocock, had moved his family to London in 1740, or thereabouts, and had settled in Shoreditch, becoming a builder and developer. His son and grandson were amongst the most active builders of Georgian London and their houses still stand in Maida Vale, Islington, Southwark, Chiswick and around Harley Street in Marylebone. John's father, George, worked with his own father in Islington and the Pocock Arms pub stands today in the Caledonian Road on what was one of their estates.

On the death of John's uncle, John Pocock, from cholera in 1832 - he is buried near his brother, George, in the churchyard of St John's Wood Chapel – his cousins were left well-to-do and his particular friend Lewis - known as 'the handsomest man in London' when young - became a patron of the arts. He founded the Art Union to popularise the visual arts, became involved in the Great Exhibition of 1851, was a pioneer of photography, collected relics of their former neighbour Dr. Samuel Johnson and discovered a number of painters who became famous, amongst them Sir John Millais. The artistic tradition widened when his son Noël married the daughter of the water-colourist, F.W. Topham, and six of their descendants became artists, or writers.

John's and Lewis's branch of the family re-rooted itself in South Africa, although John's family name died out with the death of his only son in infancy. Lewis, however, fathered the large family that lives in Africa, North America, New Zealand and England today and sometimes characteristics and looks recall shared ancestry. Reading the journals of John and Lewis, present members of the family have reason to be proud of their ancestors, who speak to them with such resolution and humour across nearly two centuries.

Tom Pocock

The Illustrations

Thanks for help with finding illustrations and for permission to reproduce them are due to Mr. Karel Schoeman, Head of Special Collections and Mrs J.A. Loos of the Iconographic Section, South African Library, Cape Town (pp. 15, 204); The Cape Archives Dept. of the State Archives, South Africa; The Elliot Collection, Cape Town (p.140); The Metropolitan Homes Trust Collection and Mr Peter B. Head (p.201); The William Fehr Collection, Cape Town (p.146); The Borough of Wandsworth (p.36); The Bishopsgate Institute (p.93); The Guildhall Library, City of London (p. 22); Grosvenor Prints (pp. 109, 161, 199); Mr Graham Christian (pp. 153, 169), Mr Hugh Watson and Professor John Pocock (p.134). The other illustrations have been provided by Lady Holder, Historical Publications and the Editor.

INDEX